D1314809

Mozart's Third Brain

Mozart's Third Brain

GÖRAN SONNEVI

TRANSLATION, PREFACE, AND NOTES

BY RIKA LESSER

FOREWORD

BY ROSANNA WARREN

YALE UNIVERSITY PRESS ■ NEW HAVEN & LONDON

A MARGELLOS
WORLD REPUBLIC OF LETTERS BOOK

The Margellos World Republic of Letters is dedicated to making literary works from around the globe available in English through translation. It brings to the English-speaking world the work of leading poets, novelists, essayists, philosophers, and playwrights from Europe, Latin America, Africa, Asia, and the Middle East to stimulate international discourse and creative exchange.

Published with assistance from the Swedish Arts Council and the Louis Stern Memorial Fund.

Set in Electra and Nobel types by Keystone Typesetting, Inc.
Printed in the United States of America.

Library of Congress Cataloging-in-Publication Data
Sonnevi, Göran, 1939–
    [Mozarts tredje hjärna. English]
    Mozart's third brain / Göran Sonnevi ; translation, preface, and notes by Rika Lesser ; foreword by Rosanna Warren.
        p.   cm. — (The Margellos world republic of letters)
    ISBN 978-0-300-14580-9 (alk. paper)
1. Sonnevi, Göran, 1939– — Translations into English. I. Lesser, Rika. II. Title.
    PT9876.29.05M6913 2009
    839.71'74—dc22   2009004608

A catalogue record for this book is available from the British Library.

This paper meets the requirements of ANSI/NISO Z39.48-1992 (Permanence of Paper).

10 9 8 7 6 5 4 3 2 1

In memory of my father
Milton S. Lesser
who focused my attention
on flowers, trees, birds, clouds,
rocks and minerals

I don't know where I
am either
I said, when you said
that you didn't know
Then you began to cry
As if trouble and sorrow were
the only reality
the only place
for life

Then you said
that I in any case was not
so unhappy
I did not
deny this

For we know
nothing
of each other's night
of each other's darkness
of each other's stars
shimmering darkly

Disparate
from *Mozart's Third Brain*

CONTENTS

FOREWORD

Göran Sonnevi has composed a massive poem that breaks almost every poetic convention—at least in the context of contemporary poetry in the United States. Hints of such disruptiveness had already appeared in his earlier selection of poems published in this country, *A Child Is Not a Knife* (1993). That volume, translated and edited by Rika Lesser, included poems from various books ranging from 1975 to 1991, and showed a poet for whom science, art, nature, ethics, politics, and love all connected in the very tissue of each poem. In the preface to that volume, Lesser quoted Göran Tunström describing Sonnevi's ambition to write "a single long poem, a commentary on everything that comes within range of his language." And the last poem in *A Child Is Not a Knife*, "Burge, Öja; 1989," from Sonnevi's most recent book at that date, eddied in seven dense pages, demanding of the reader a high tolerance for abstraction and cosmic speculation: "I approach the edge / of integration, death   What will I see when I get there? Will song be / possible there too?" But for the most part, *A Child's* elliptical, even crystalline lyrics sufficiently resembled the Postwar Lyric International Style to gain an immediate hearing from North American readers. Its audience, we might say, was ready-made. *Mozart's Third Brain* presents a different case.

"We enter into the infinite brain," the speaker claims in XXXII, and that well may be the sensation of the reader entering this book. It is partly a question of scale. Sonnevi has fanned out in long lines, long sections, and a total architecture of 144 sections. In topics, too, he has gone out of his way to offend; the poem worries away at every subject proscribed from polite conversation—and from the tacitly polite conversation that dominates a certain mode of the "spiritual," "personal" North American poem. *Mozart's Third Brain* ponders not just politics but current events—the atrocious and not-so-atrocious events current, we could even say coursing, during the composition of the poem, including the siege of Sarajevo, the massacre of Bosnian Muslim men at Srebrenica, and the Hutu genocide of Tutsis in Rwanda. And not just current events but an even more unwieldy subject, economics, evoking "The sea of finance capital, of over 7 trillion dollars, / moving freely over the surface of the globe" (XI). As if this weren't sufficiently heavy weather, the poem also wants to talk—and "talk" is often the operative word—about philosophy (Parmenides and Heraclitus), difficult music (Schoenberg, Ligeti), and, God help us, mathematics (stochastics, probability . . .). It seems a recipe for disaster. In what sense, one may ask, does this book constitute a poem?

Here begins the adventure. In *Mozart's Third Brain* Sonnevi reinvents the long poem and reinvents poetic language. What threatens to sprawl, or to squander itself in random Op-Ed notations, turns out to engage in a disciplined quest to integrate private consciousness—expressed here in the character "I"—into wider and wider connections between the natural world (rocks, plants, and weather); the emotional world of friendship, family, and erotic love; and the political realm. "We seek the order," the voice announces in XXXIX.

The mathematics of randomness provides a loose model for the search. In stochastic processes, the next state of a system is not completely determined by the present and past states of the system. The theory of stochastics describes and calculates the patterns latent in random events. Sonnevi also relies on the notion of "self-organization" as a formal principle for his poem: the spontaneous rise of complex structures out of tiny fluctuations in a dynamic energy flow. Sonnevi engages the reader in the search for the form of the poem he is in the process of composing by making that search identical with "our" lives and with our consciousness of our lives:

> In music
>
> proportions accumulate, in whirling numeric relations,

nor do they become visible, until

afterwards, stochastically, out of the quantity of signals . . .

We are *that* language; also *that* music, in its third coming

Then we, too, go into the ordered night (VI)

As *The Divine Comedy*, in its first two lines, associates the personal quest of the pilgrim ("I found myself in a dark wood") with the communal pilgrimage of life ("In the middle of the journey of our life"), so Sonnevi connects the personal quest in his poem with ever more complex versions of the communal. The search for its own form drives *Mozart's Third Brain*, but that impulse cannot be separated from the search for justice or, as Sonnevi names it, the Greek Dike.

The poem digs into its own meanings:

only if I dare go deeper

What is deeper?

That I can find out only

by going deeper

The answer to Pilate's question

—so pursues XV, in its pursuit of that famous question "What is truth?" (John 18:38). Truth, for Sonnevi, is revealed in evolving form, in the very principle of its dynamism. "We are in the deepening architecture, its folds of light, its / construction and destruction   Fold is laid against fold," proclaims XXV, describing its own behavior.

Sonnevi needed the notion of stochastics to accommodate a high degree of accident in the material and progress of his poem. As it unfolds, in its "fold against fold"— which is, among other things, an image of the physical organ of the brain—it takes in personal incident and observation, the deaths of friends in the real time of composition, and the assault of daily global television news. At the same time the poem aspires to a condition of timeless, redemptive vision, and has, at times, a fiery Hölderlinian temper. Since it has ruled out a theological solution to the problem of senseless suffering, it borrows a mathematical and structural one, which is also musical, in imagining an order that can absorb and finally organize into symbolic form a set of random documentary data (as "a wagtail walks on the grass," I, and "On television / yesterday two small children who had been shot lay, like bloody dolls, on a bench, / pictures from Sarajevo," VI). The poem wants, that is, to convert noise to music. Though Mozart presides as the ultimate synthesis of grief and joy, it takes *Mozart's Third Brain* its full 144 sections to work out the terms of its own difficult music. And why "third" brain? The poem seems to provide many hints of answers to that occult question—more than I can lay out here. But one suggestion arises in CIV, and seems to pertain to the left brain–right brain thesis, with a further notion of a transcendent "third" mode of cognition to which music gives access: "Mozart in the first brain; in the resounding second: music / We are in the excluded third, impossibly, in the counterpart." Which hearkens back to a yearning manifest in an earlier poem, "Dyrön, 1981," in *A Child Is Not a Knife:* "a third term must exist; it cannot // exist in language; or perhaps: // in language alone."

As soon as we touch on the matter of *verbal* music, the reader ignorant of Swedish acknowledges that he or she is entirely in the hands of the translator. We are lucky, in this case, to have Rika Lesser as our guide. Not only has she been translating Göran Sonnevi's poems for years, and not only is she herself a strong poet, but she works closely with Sonnevi, whose English is excellent. To the extent that any poem can find itself in another language, we may trust *Mozart's Third Brain* in English as a performance of the Swedish. Language, in this tormented poem, is both theme and *prima materia*. "How am I to exist in this shattered / human language," asks the speaker in XXVIII. And in the key section LXVI he states:

> We are in the perpetually damaged language   And will
> remain there, so as not to become monsters   That's where

the given is broken and new form becomes possible
I hear new birds   The song thrush sings
at the break of day

This passage is characteristic of Sonnevi. It moves fluidly from speculative abstraction to a private act of perception and insists, by juxtaposition, that the speculation ("the perpetually damaged language," "new form becomes possible") and the perception ("new birds") reflect each other. The idea of breakage links the abstraction ("the given") and the physical surround ("the break of day"). Why is the language damaged? Because *we* are damaged, in our humanness; because we are not gods; because, as this poem painstakingly records, we shuffle around in our games of power, hurting each other; because we love; and because we love those who die, and will die ourselves. A language that refuses to idealize and instead, in its intense Swedish earnestness, keeps looking for truth will have to live and work in the damages, so that we do not "become monsters." That is, so that we accept our humanness and that of others, without imposing murderously abstract and utopian solutions on our fellow humans. The poem has taught us to read "the given" that is broken and the "new form" that becomes possible as both poetic and political renovation. That analogy is made explicit a few lines further on in the passage where "On television we see / the political elites, their awkward dance."

When *Mozart's Third Brain* was published in Sweden in 1996, its anxiety about the destruction of the natural world, its premonition that "the economies can burst at any time" (CXXXII), and its demand for justice for the victims of ethnic cleansing had a certain resonance. But in 2009, as we witness a world financial system reeling in a way that seemed inconceivable to hotheaded investors and lenders even a few months ago, and as Radovan Karadzic has finally been arrested to stand trial in The Hague for crimes against humanity, Sonnevi's poem has an eerie urgency and timeliness. It makes us watch TV, and absorb a daily quantity of horrors. It ponders the distancing effects of such non-knowledge delivered as images on a screen. It ponders our help-lessness, and it makes a dynamic form out of that pondering. One of its most often repeated words, "abyss," looms as the antithesis to the drive toward form, and as the poem unfolds, it records a contest between abyss and a unifying architecture of conscious experience: "We are the thresholds   That which is form inside us / is born, like the unknown child   Then we watch over it" (CXXXVII).

Even as Sonnevi strains to give birth to poetic form in the light of atrocity ("We stand in the sheen of the blinding knife," XLI), he leads the reader through the dying of several close friends, so we experience the blinding knife as the fact of personal loss as well as the bewildering news of genocide. Those individual acts of mourning (for Bengt Anderson, Karl Vennberg, Anna Rydstedt—the names come to seem impor-tant) save the poem from too heavy a cargo of abstraction. We participate imagina-tively in those lives, those deaths. The poem lures us, step by step, to suffer, to care, to mourn, and to live in an enlarged state of awareness. So large, finally, that it brings microcosm together with macrocosm, and brokenness together with wholeness, in a visionary ending that does not really end. The image of the egg contains both whole-ness and brokenness, the universe and a tiny individual instance. Whatever Mozart's first and second brains were (harmony? drama?), "Mozart's third brain is unfinished, I grasp this over and over again," the speaker tells us in CXLI, almost at the end of the poem. The poem concludes in a dash, which leaves the work of consciousness, perpetually unfinished, to continue within the brain of the reader. In this majestic, original, and painful poem, Göran Sonnevi has released a new form of fertility into the world:

> On the path in the woods lies a small blue egg, speckled brown,
> broken   On one part of the inside, where the white membrane no longer is,
> it shines clear blue, in its inner vault   Here the song ends—

> Rosanna Warren

THE RETROSPECTIVE MONTAGE, RESUMED

More than fifteen years have elapsed since A *Child Is Not a Knife: Selected Poems of Göran Sonnevi* (Princeton, 1993) was published; it is still in print. Before that time, the only separate edition of Sonnevi's work in English was a bilingual chapbook translated by Robert Bly: *The Economy Spinning Faster and Faster* (Sun, 1982). It was not my intention to become Sonnevi's sole English-language translator, but it seems I have assumed that role since the mid-1980s. As his work and international reputation have grown and spread, respectively, it has been a great honor and a tremendous responsibility virtually to remain so.

Because Sonnevi's oeuvre is, in some sense, one long poem that continues from book to book, I hope the reader will turn or return to A *Child Is Not a Knife*. My preface to that book includes a section bearing the title "Sonnevi: A Translator's Retrospective Montage." I mean to carry on from there, with some variation. Updated bibliographical information follows the Notes; biographical sketches of author and translator follow the Acknowledgments to the poem.

Sonnevi's wide-ranging language seeks out everything it can possibly grasp. Rosanna Warren perceives some disjunction between the "elliptical, even crystalline lyrics" I translated in A *Child Is Not a Knife* and the longer-lined sections of *Mozart's Third Brain* as it "reinvents poetic language." To one whose ear has not been trained on the Swedish originals read in the poet's voice, this chasm may well be larger on the page than the stage. In my earlier Montage I wrote of how hearing Sonnevi read aloud utterly changed my view of his work. I would not have translated his poetry if I had not heard him read. I also explained that I translate the poems so that he can comfortably read them aloud in English. We have always agreed on the overriding importance of rhythm in translation. If you are reading him in my English, vocalizing or not, you should know that the poet's voice addresses you as *du*, the form that is singular and familiar, individual and intimate.

Sonnevi's work, in all its aspects, still simultaneously goes straight to one's heart and head. Working on and with this poet for nearly twenty-five years has become no less challenging. We continually argue over words and concepts in Swedish and English. We also laugh. As stated in "Whose life? you asked" from *Poems with No Order* (1983):

> It makes no difference
> There's nothing but
> you, and you
> Only when you become explicit,
> when you
> question me, and I
> answer, when there's
> an exchange   Only then is there language
> only then are we human
>
> from *A Child Is Not a Knife*, 15

Now's the Time—30 August 2008
Third Thoughts Approaching Mozart's Third Brain

I am well aware that many or possibly most readers never give any thought to the translators of the books they read. There are translators who believe the highest compliment they can be paid is that readers failed to notice their existence while reading their work. As reader, writer, and translator, I am ecstatic when I disappear into a literary text; reading can be an egoless act, sometimes of radical identification.

But the product of the act of translation is never the work of a single author, and this fact should never go unacknowledged. A responsible reader bears this in mind, not only for the sake of what gets "lost" in translation but also because of additions, adulterations, embellishments, excisions—whether intentional or unconscious on the "faithful" translator's part—to say nothing of misunderstandings, or that which may truly be inexpressible, or so much harder to express in one of the languages in play.

In any case, *Mozart's Third Brain* is no easy read, neither intellectually nor emotionally. Humanly and humanely, however, the reader will encounter in the poem the same pleasures and problems he or she confronts in daily life on this planet. I offer an excerpt from XIV as an example:

> What is a nation? What is Swedishness? As if these
> questions themselves had led to murder   The territorial instinct, the earth
> out of which one is born, perhaps the earth of the grave, the earth of one's
> father and mother; *dulce et decorum est pro patria mori,*
> no, dammit! I saw pictures from Ravensbrück, and from
> other camps   The same sorts of faces as those from Bosnia and Somalia
> The faces of suffering and starvation   Are all images
> executioners' images? No! But every image is utterly excluded
> Living things, agents of the invisible god, they are
>   not images
> Once I believed images were our children; but that's not
>   true either
> Every child has its own perfect face   In whatever
>   transformation of suffering or joy
> it may find itself   Every face is of earth   We are the one earth
> Our pact with the murderers, how does it look? Faces
>   turned away; earth averted

2 August 2008—Second Thoughts

A Long Backward Glance: December 1991–August 1999

Göran Sonnevi and I have continued to keep up an unusual working relationship. We go over just about every word in every line of every poem of his I translate into English. In the 1980s we wrote letters, by hand or typewriter. Without the support of various foundations (please see the Acknowledgments) we could never have begun or completed either of these books. In the spring of 1999 in Stockholm we went over the first twenty-four sections of "Mozart's Third Brain," supplementing frequent face-to-face meetings with phone conversations. On returning to New York with "final drafts," I issued an ultimatum: "You must get a computer if this translation is to go on." I still have his "first e-mail ever," dated 29 August 1999.

Although we have corresponded in this way for many years, only in the last decade did I learn that when I receive poems in manuscript—no matter whether forty pages or four hundred—I am expected to drop everything, read them instantly, and give Göran my thoughts. . . . When we are discussing something—word, phrase, concept— at the point where one of us is about to implode or explode (I noticed this in Stockholm in June) I suggest something entirely different, or simply start to laugh. Skill or stratagem, I believe this benefit has accrued with my continuing practice of tai chi chuan, a martial art that requires a great deal of mental focus. In any case, I always have the last word, in English.

In *A Child Is Not a Knife*, I presented what struck me then as an essential selection of work from books Sonnevi had published between 1975 and 1991. The poems came from volumes whose English titles would be *The Impossible* (1975), *Poems with No Order* (1981), *Unfinished Poems* (1987), and *The Tree* (1991). In the final section of *A Child*'s Montage, dated 1 December 1991, I wrote about the title poem of the 1991 collection, published on 8 November, a poem just over seventy-five pages long: "After one reading of 'The Tree,' I told him in August, 'Life is too short; there's no danger of my ever translating *that* poem.' But having spent the last two weeks *in* 'The Tree,' I only wonder now how and when I will manage to translate it."

I did not translate *that* poem. Five years later I was given the manuscript of *Mozart's Third Brain*, Sonnevi's thirteenth book of poems, published in Sweden in November 1996, which consists of two parts: "*Disparates*" (so named after Goya's etchings and aquatints, sometimes called "Follies"), about a hundred pages of discrete, primarily short, lyric poems, and the circa-two-hundred-page title poem, a suite of 144 sections that bear roman numerals. In 1996–97 I translated perhaps a dozen of the *Disparates*. From then on, although I occasionally rendered some of his older or newer poems, translating the long, meditative, visionary title poem was my chief concern; it was completed in June 2003. More than 120 of its sections have appeared in print or electronic journals to date. The book you have in your hands is not identical with the Swedish volume; it is merely (merely!) the title poem. Here are brief quotations from several Swedish reviews contemporary with the first publication of the Swedish edition:

- All the poetry Göran Sonnevi has written in these last three decades is a gigantic and wholly unique building under construction that rises up above the landscape of Swedish poetry. *Mozart's Third Brain* makes this construct tower even higher.
  —Lennart Sjögren in *Östgöta Correspondenten*
- Göran's Sonnevi's work will come to be read as a uniquely multifaceted testimony concerning what it was like to attempt to live a conscientious and dignified life on the fringe of Europe during the second half of the twentieth century. . . . *Mozart's Third Brain* is a collection of poetry that is in every respect a great work.
  —Mona Sandqvist in *Svenska Dagbladet*

- It is remarkable that year after year Göran Sonnevi can follow the world's "permanent murders" and nonetheless write about them almost in journal form. He revises everything, trying to understand and interpret. How many of us manage just now to allow our thoughts seriously to be influenced by the fate of people fleeing destruction in the jungles of Zaire?

  —Sigvard Lindqvist in *Jönköpings-Postens/Smålands Allehanda*

- To read Göran Sonnevi is to allow oneself to become incorporated in a dialogue, a discussion, a recitation of Mass; and as at Mass one allows the words to work as rhythm and sound, simultaneously attending his speech, listening to what he says. For he speaks with intensity and wisdom about what is urgent to him, and with an enormously strong demand that the hearer, the receiver actually listen. He makes what is said a necessity that has the same dignity as all things that sustain life.

  —Arne Johnsson in *Bonniers Litterära Magasin*

Although historical or political aspects of Sonnevi's work are often remarked—Lennart Sjögren, quoted above, writes in the same review: "Even in his early work, Göran Sonnevi had to shoulder the weight of being the conscience of the Western world"—the literary, musical, artistic, philosophical, and meditative aspects are equally marked. Again to quote Mona Sandqvist (who wrote a dissertation on Sonnevi): "The musical harmony of many voices is a kind of emblem for Sonnevi's contrapuntal way of writing. The voices of others constantly make themselves heard in his text. They form a latticework of hidden and open allusion to Plato, Pindar, Dante, Dostoyevsky, Rilke, Hölderlin, Pound, Almqvist, Ekelöf, Nelly Sachs, and countless other interlocutors."

12 August 2008—The Continuum

> The fragment of the Brain draws nearer   *Cerebri substantia*
> Also in its complete abstraction   Derivative   Or its
> resonant information, from I-don't-know-which topologies
> *Hyperouranios topos*   In its non-existent infinity   I hear
> the music   That which cannot end   That which nonetheless has an end
> from Mozart's Third Brain, CXXXIV

After all these years, will my work on *Mozart's Third Brain* come to an end? How long has it been? It took four years to translate the poem, another six to find the right publisher and come to terms; the date of my contract with Yale University Press coincides with my fifty-fifth birthday. *Mozart's Third Brain* is a highly empirical poem and, as we know, "Rome wasn't built . . ."

Leave me in medias res then, for there is nowhere else, no other place, to be, as Sonnevi continues to live and write. Even if I cannot keep this one long poem or indeed all his work in mind at once (as I had once, at twenty, turned my brain into something like a concordance for Rainer Maria Rilke's poetry and plays, before there was one), as I continue to live and work with it, I can see the universe of the work, better, more clearly. Not quite the Ouroboros, but as some long, thickening snake. Or a lacertine. Etched on a rock or a mountain—Swedish *berg* means both. In the sky. Touching everything, everyone. Inside and out. Coiling, looping, stretching, contracting. In all directions, all dimensions. At once.

δ

First Backward Step—Spring/Summer 1984

An untitled poem from *Poems with No Order* (1983) begins:

Summer has turned now   And I go
deeper inside my mother   She who
bears me, ceaselessly, all
the more deeply into the motion of growth
Wild roses bloom on the mountain
The birds' voices have changed, cry warnings,
the voices of their young, more delicate   Mary
's keys blossom, along-
side night-scented orchids, there
in the narrow glade   In the lake
girls bathe in white suits   I
walk by in wooden shoes, my footing uncertain
I think about the unfinished, the construction
of what is, which is also
the world, as an aspect of this building
that also is born from my mother, as she too
is a part of the growing, and
of the dying; for if death were not
everything soon would be finished

It contains virtually everything I love best about Sonnevi's poetry: the precision of the natural scene, its motion—a rhythmic rocking from line to line ("out of the cradle endlessly"), the critical enjambments, which had to be mirrored in the translation, the movement toward or into mathematics and philosophy, Sonnevi's deep uncertainty of everything but the unfinished. This mother in whom "there are no contradictions" never speaks, never answers, but we must, it is our responsibility. Toward the end of the poem we are told:

> Because if we did not speak, if all creation—each being
> and thing in existence—did not speak, neither would she
> exist   She would not know of her own existence
> For she sees her child   When her dark eyes see her child
> even her invisibility quickens   I know that
> she also looks at us with the eyes of judgment, straight through
> the underworld down to the bottom of Hell   To that which under-
> lies Hell   She prays for us, the doomed   She alone and no
> other   The luminous night fills with the night orchid's scent   Moths
> are still awake, while the birds sleep, a short time
> In deepest Hell all are awake   The stars spiral, turn,
> join in dance   The great eyes are dark now, and still

"Summer has turned now" was the first poem by Göran Sonnevi I translated; it took perhaps six months. An essay I wrote about translating it appeared in *Translating Poetry: The Double Labyrinth*, edited by Daniel Weissbort (Iowa, 1989). Reflecting further on this short, individual (Sonnevi uses the word "freestanding"), and yet *essential* poem, I see that a couple of other key words are missing, notably "song" and "music." But "dance" is present, and it is on equal terms with them and with life. You will see and hear a great deal of whirling, eddying, and turning take place in Sonnevi's poetry, done by stars, water, wind, waves, even living things, each with its under-current of spiral energy.

Summer turns at one solstice. Near the other, equally breathtaking natural scenes occur in Sonnevi's winter landscapes. In *Mozart's Third Brain*, written between 3 July 1992 and 12 June 1996, there are quite a few of both.

δ

δδ

Second Backward Step—Retrogression to 1974–75

In "Sonnevi: A Translator's Retrospective Montage" (*A Child*, xix), I mentioned reading some of Sonnevi's work, possibly giving the impression that when I lived for a year in Sweden I had read *The Impossible* (1975), a book of more than four hundred pages. This was not possible: I lived there from one August to the next; the book came out in November. But Sonnevi *was* all the rage, for in February 1974 his *Poems, 1959–1973*, appeared, a collection of his six previous volumes. Books and their title poems are easily confused; moreover, Sonnevi's 1972 volume, *The Unfinished Language*, opened with a short poem called "The Impossible."

The Impossible itself is divided into two segments; the first consists of individual poems under the heading "Unfinished"; the second is a single long poem that bears the title "The Impossible; Second Part." In 1987, Sonnevi publishes a volume of freestanding poems he titles *Unfinished Poems*, whose second segment continues in his next collection, *The Tree*, published in 1991. Back among *The Impossible*'s individual "Unfinished" poems are two sequences that prefigure *Mozart's Third Brain* (book, poem, phrase). To back into lost time and reveal the essential unity of the "one long poem that continues from book to book," here are three sections from *The Impossible* (1975).

MOZART VARIATIONS; SECOND PART

147

It has its starting point
in music,
        the
music that we have in common—

For music is greater than our selves

There are faces
that come toward me out of the darkness
out of the darkness of the past
and the darkness of the future

Each face
has its voice   And beneath the skin
a swarm of voices,
the intense voices of others

The voice from the darkness is singing

What is it singing?

I am a crack, an ooz-
ing wound   I am
an April day, dry, with
blue air, water   The trees

gray, intense   Under dry
leaves on the ground life goes
on, insects, small mammals
calling to one another
Hepaticas look at one another with their
eyes   Wood anemones burn in the darkness

I am here to sing in a voice that is
utterly clear   I am
water, air, space   I am everything
one needs   I am one
voice among
many   Now the gray branches'
buds are opening   Now
the green bark
under the gray is
widening   Now water is running
through the opened
ground, from the spring, down
the slope
The shrew hears me and answers
in its most delicate
voice

I can dance too, entirely
alone between the trees
No one sees me, except
the birds, the hepaticas

and the small
mammals under the leaves
I fling myself between the trees'
slender trunks, myself invisible
as the thin layer of light
around their bark—

One after another the voices go silent   It is night
Then the quick flashes of light
awaken
beneath the thin
membrane of sleep
Dance most swift, whirling, giddying
in an infinity of time
in a space without end
entirely of the senses
The face of the voices
returns unknown

THE IMPOSSIBLE; SECOND PART
256

Crush the impossible!

It ex-
ists, and we cannot escape
The impossible's
enormous, four-dimensional crystal,

expanded

straight through all of

reality

Even inside

the architecture

of bodies

The lives of beings

throughout history

beyond

all of it, inside

all of it

Crush the flowing impossible!

Dash the rock

against the child!

THE IMPOSSIBLE; SECOND PART

257

rose of the human

rose of fire

Whirling, it opens

with one

petal for

every human

Each and every

petal of this rose

has the same name

∞

13 August 2008—Self-examination

Do you understand Mozart's Third Brain?

That question is one I had put to many Swedish readers—especially when I first read the book. I asked everyone I knew, close friends of the poet's, members of the Swedish Academy, acquaintances of mine who are among his broad readership. Swedish people are extremely good at being silent; the verb *tiga* denotes actively keeping silent.

About the phrase itself, I have both ideas and doubts. About the title poem and the whole Swedish book my own answer is that I understand it more with each reading, but not completely. Every time I read it over I get something more out of it.

How many times have you read it?

I have no idea. One hundred, several hundred, a thousand. The whole thing right straight through, half a dozen or so. When I read proofs I'll read it through a few more times, probably with recognition more than comprehension.

How many times have you read it with comprehension?

The last time I read it straight through to write this Montage I understood it better than before. And the time before that better than the preceding time. The best analogy I can draw is with discovering improvement, after months or years of practice, at the sequence in tai chi form known as "Step Back and Repulse Monkey," which involves stepping backward while aiming one's gaze (and intention) forward and at an angle, rotating 180 degrees at the waist, and opening out to the opposite side. ("Opening out" is in reference to elaborate arm movements, too complex to describe fully here.) Then one steps back with the opposite leg and so on. I further associate this progress in backward movement and forward intention with the following excerpt that invokes recursive functions, from section XIII of *Mozart's Third Brain*:

> I prepare myself for language's breaking out
> into a larger space   To a more complete music
> That's what I imagine! But I can never know in
> advance   I only know that I cannot turn
> > back,
> that I cannot look back   Recursive
> functions are something else; every re-
> > entry
> occurs in the future   Participates, thus, in oblivion—

Having read and reread the brain in whole or parts for nearly a dozen years, I have been living inside it. I am beginning to emerge, to step outside of it. In more ways than one.

14 August 2008—Personal Connections & Beyond

> *The living have the right to mistakes   The dead cannot make any*
> *But the dead have the right to demand we do right by them,*
> *that we take care of them   That we show them our sorrow and our love*
> > *from "Palinode" in* The Tree

In *Mozart's Third Brain* Sonnevi addresses and commemorates people named (for example, Anna R, Smail Hodzic, Arnold Schoenberg) and unnamed (among these are his parents and victims of the Holocaust and of other genocides), as well as a handful designated only by initials (T, V, B, G, H, J). Some of these I had encountered "in real life" before meeting Göran. Over the years I got to know others through him.

Bengt Anderson in particular became a dear friend (see note to XXV). He lived in Jonsered, in a wooden house very near the Villa Furuborg, where Rilke was the guest of the Gibsons, friends of Ellen Key, in 1904. The first time I set off to meet Bengt, I traveled with my sole American friend in Sweden at the time, Gina Riddle, who wrote the date on the back of photos she took that day, almost exactly twenty-four years ago: 16 *August 1984.* We concealed a kilo of fresh shrimp from Göteborg's Feskekörka and a bottle of white wine in a book bag. Our bus arrived early. At first we all loudly pretended not to recognize one another; there was virtually no one else at the kiosk where the bus stopped. At the time I was the only person on the west coast of Sweden with long, nearly black hair and red plastic eyeglass frames. Bengt asked if we wanted the Rilke tour or the mill tour first. We replied we would soon be soaked and stinking of spoiled shrimp. . . . At home with Bengt and Maj, I explained that my own first book was a selection of Rilke's poems entitled *Holding Out.* No, I was not "holding out" on them; this was a gesture, a wish the poet expressed for the young suicide toward the end of his "Requiem for Wolf Graf von Kalckreuth":

> If only you had *once*
> seen how Fate enters into verses
> and does not return, how it becomes image there,
> and nothing but image, just as an ancestor
> in the frame, when sometimes you look up,
> seems to resemble you, and again bears no resemblance—:
> you should have held out.
>
> . . . .
>
> Who speaks of triumph? Surviving is everything.

Then we saw the villa and we walked to "Aspen, gray, the lake Rilke also looked out over, / most likely, when he completed *Orpheus. Eurydike. Hermes*" (XXX). Visiting the Andersons at Lilla Furuborg became a ritual. We often talked about poetry and music, including Göran's poetry. Little did I suspect, that first time, how much Bengt and I would come to share as survivors.

+

Göran is very protective of other people's privacy, especially that of friends. But we agreed that I could identify "T," whom the general Swedish reader will easily recognize as the illustrious, universally acclaimed, and beloved poet Tomas Tranströmer. I wrote of him in my earlier Montage but did not reveal there that I first met Tomas in New York City when I had been studying Swedish for perhaps a year. I heard him read in English at the Manhattan Theater Club, most likely in the spring of 1973. During my senior year at Yale (1973–74), I began translating poems from his book *Stigar* (Paths, 1973). In August, young Amy Lowell Travelling Poet-Scholar that I was, I arranged to visit him and his family in Västerås, returning to Göteborg from Helsinki. His wife, Monica, nursed me through a very bad cold. Tomas turns up with some frequency in *Mozart's Third Brain*, always in contexts involving music. See, for example, XXX, or C, from which the excerpt below comes. In November 1990 he suffered a massive stroke, as a result of which he became partially paralyzed and mostly aphasic. Nonetheless, he has published several books since that time.

Memories

move   Even in brains that are totally destroyed   *Hvairneins stads*, I read
in the Gothic lexicon, the Place of a Skull, kraniou topos   Everyone's
brains re-created, exponentially   Crystal   Crystal   As if everything were
growing clarity, darkness   The brain in its flight, in a universal form
T and I conversed   Questions   Answers   The house of memories grew
    On the radio
a symphonic poem of Sibelius, *The Oceanides*   A kind of birth music
Before what?   Reminiscent of the symphonic prelude to the concluding
sequence in Schoenberg's Gurrelieder, I said, and T nodded   On a paper
napkin he had written the year 1914, the year Sibelius composed the piece

T appears in many other parts of the long poem that continues from book to book, but you may have to learn Swedish to read these passages yourself.

Tomas Tranströmer was the guest of honor at WALTIC, the first Writers' and Literary Translators' International Congress, organized by the Swedish Writers Union, held in Stockholm from 29 June to 2 July. With Monica Tranströmer I read aloud one of his poems, from *The Wild Market Square* (1983), that I translated for the occasion:

THE STATION

A train has rolled in. Railroad car after car stands here,
but no doors open, no one gets off or on.
Are there any doors at all? Inside there it's swarming
with shut-ins, people moving round and around
They stare out through windows that won't be budged.

Outside a man with a sledgehammer walks alongside the train.
He strikes the wheels, faintly they toll. Everywhere but here!
Here the sound swells inconceivably: lightning striking,
the clang of a cathedral bell, a sound that circumnavigates the globe
lifting the whole train and the terrain's wet stones.
Everything sings. You will remember this. Fare on!

Participating in a Best Practices Session at the congress, I attempted to address an increasingly trying situation: being approached by poets or other interested parties who wish to translate Sonnevi's poetry from my English translations alone, people who have no knowledge of Swedish and no intention of learning the language. When I talk to general readers about such things they look at me in disbelief.

+

The initial that stands in for my existence is an ink drop in the long "title" poem that follows some 170 pages of shorter *Disparates* in *The Ocean* (2005). This is the volume that brought Sonnevi the 2006 Nordic Council Prize; the title poem itself runs just under 250 pages. This excerpt runs from pages 271 to 272:

September 11th, 2001

I read an e-mail from R, about the attack on the World Trade Center
rush downstairs to the TV, see the burning towers, smoke sweeping up toward
Brooklyn, where R is   While I am watching this come reports
of the attack on the Pentagon   In replay I see images of the airplanes,
hijacked passenger planes, flown directly into the enormous towers, where
50,000 people work   I write back to R, tell her
to stay indoors, not to inhale the smoke   In succession come images
of the bleeding and wounded emerging from the ruins, all are covered
    with dust
The telephone lines to New York are blocked, I try to put a call through
A reply from R, who had walked to the Brooklyn Heights Promenade, looked
    out toward
Manhattan sheathed in smoke, the buildings visible only as shadows
    White soot
falling over her, her eyes stinging   She goes to a friend's studio; he is
frightened   She tries to call her mother   Who, I think, can see this
from her window in an eldercare residence   I write about *Besy*—evil spirits,
Demons, which R is reading now—these were the ancestors   Later I see
    pictures
from Nablus or East Jerusalem of Palestinians dancing in the streets
One of them says: This is candy from Osama bin Laden   I write

this to R too; compare it with the Palestinian rejoicing during Saddam
    Hussein's
missile attacks on Israel   In the night there are rocket strikes on Kabul;
    presumably
by the opposition, whose leader, Massoud, was the target of a suicide bomber
the day before, still unknown whether he's alive   Is there a connection?
    R writes
she will go to a church, or to the synagogue, to pray   Although she
doesn't really know how   I answer, we have to do that, each in his own
                way, if we can
A fourth hijacked passenger plane has crashed in Pennsylvania   The number
        of dead in New York and Washington still unknown
            from "The Ocean; *Disparate Infinito*"

Having whirled so long in the Brain's convolutions, this is the one passage from his latest book's title poem I have dipped my quill into, myself long mute (as a poet) about that day here at home. Only in arriving at "Manhattan sheathed in smoke" last month for "*Manhattan täckt av rök*"—which my Swedish friend did not experience firsthand—have I finally found words to describe what I saw then.

I have translated a dozen or more of *The Ocean*'s individual *Disparates*, its briefer "follies."

I doubt I shall ever undertake translating the long one in its entirety. That would seem infinite folly.

Ω

Coda—16 August 2008

Paul Valéry maintained: "A poem is never finished, only abandoned."

Our tai chi sifu reminds us of three things: "Practice, patience, perseverance."

Perfection there is none.

Gunnar Ekelöf in "The Devil's Sermon": "If something perfect existed, there would be no perfection."

We give ourselves up to these conditions. They are unconditional.

Rika Lesser

Mozart's Third Brain

I

Nothing is unaltered in a brain   No more
than in some other landscape, geological strata,
trees that grow, the children's slide, gleaming
through the mythical ash trees, no longer a creamy green, some

now

withering in the summer drought   A wagtail walks on the grass
The row of alders obscures the rock   Last night the moon, a cres-

cent,

rose over Valfjället, I can't recall now whether waxing
or waning . . .   The light of the sky was encompassing, just as I

remembered it,

unchanged, though I know this cannot be

so

As if we all nonetheless were in the matrix of the one, womb-like,

contained within it,

simultaneously existing and non-existing, if

we can believe

the logic of *Parmenides*, which I'm not so sure about
The brain's not a digital computer, so I've gathered
from what I've read, as well as from personal experience . . .
Someone drives by on the road in a freight moped   People
are not the same, nor am I, in some odd sort of

permanence

For a long time I've known that the Parmenides-Heraclitus dichotomy
doesn't hold up either   And that the one is not the

excluded third term, nor is it the unknown, in a desperate
formalization
Everything is touch, close by the maternal, in sexual
dichotomy
In the morning I touch you, cautiously, without
coming toward
you
I have also touched others, innocently, when you weren't
looking

II

Now music resounds inside me   Mozart again; but also all of
the others
Even Brahms, and Verdi, who are otherwise strange to me . . .
Now the grass, the foliage, fling me out, into what
is not despair
I love the beings and things all around me, close by   The ones
that also touch me;
you, whom I love, I touch incessantly . . .
But not in a continuum; irretrievably, we are two, parts,
even if of each other, in our loci, un-confused . . .

In the hush of the luminous night the sound of the sea is audible, a
distant sound, that I too now think I can hear,
if I listen   During the day we were on islands
in the archipelago, all the grass scorched, the sheep

sharply outlined against the rocks and the sky   A green
scarab flew droning through the rock cleft   The little
rowboat we use is lovely, a direct descendant
of the dragon ship's form   I rowed too, for almost
the first time since childhood, the first time in the sea
Hard to balance the wind, and the waves, from the second
                                                        seat

We swam in the sea, naked, then we had coffee, shared
                              a butter cake three ways
I stubbed my toe on the rock when I kicked off my slacks;
                    now it's black and blue, hurts a little
The moon *is* waxing, almost half; I thought of Yeats, his
                                                        system
of classification, for people, wondered as to
whether every system, however false it may be
gives off some kind of knowledge; for the fragmented does not
                                                        exist;
in any case not outside the invisible matrix

III

Every system *is* false; once I used this
                              knowledge
as a partial apology for Marxism, even though I recognized
the systematic misrepresentation   That's how things are;
at least half our knowledge is always repressed

I look at the cracks in women's genitals, the pubic hair beside the slit
is thicker

bushier   I look at my own sex, shield it
from

the sun   All genital skin is somewhat darker, more
pigmented

What are we protecting? The invisible matrix   The one
whose name we may not utter;

and about which we can say nothing   The cloud of
the absence of knowledge;

to allude to one of the names of concealment . . .

Music covers us with skin, touches us with skin

We are painfully described there, even in great delight

In Bartók's music for strings, percussion and celesta

the long fugue slowly grows up toward an unheard-of, an immense plateau

and rests there, in immensity   I heard this a long time ago

And find it again now; as if it had been forgotten; as if it

had not rested in the one, the one in its growth   How to measure that growth?

You can't   It rests in the underworld of paradoxes, where

every argument is identical with its opposite, endlessly repeated

Against this there is only music   And it is music that supports
the unending construction of the all

The plateau is like the sea; as if the sea were resting in its inversion, upward . . .

Then it all can begin   We live our lives, split, against one another,
with one another, dynamically—

IV

The flute played microtonally, as if of its own accord . . .
In *Parmenides* I read about the contacts between
numbers, in the one, that the contacts are always fewer by one   Then
I had an image, of the brain's plurality, where the contacts, *hapseis*,
were ever increasing, constantly growing, and how this irrevocably alters
the image of every unity, or the non-image, in the imageless, because
the simple structures of language do not suffice . . .

Before me on the desk is a small female head
made of bronze, which I also looked at yesterday   In the evening I
                                                    learned
it was made by Torsten Renqvist; all at once my vision was trans-
                                                    formed
Another world of forms arose   I had seen
a small Syrian sculpture, thin, made of clay, a woman with
the beak of a bird, big eyes   I said: how eager she looks, as
                                                    if
she were still searching for something, after four thousand years, and
                                                    had not
                                                    found it

Inside I'm uneasy, nervous   Anxiously I follow
the reciprocal movements of empires, those to come, those
extant, or those already dead   In the media we are
a new kind of conversation, quick as a flash, often nervous
But we're not the instantaneous, *to exaiphnes,* that constitutes

the one, the continuum, non-existing, among all
entities, in time, space, or in pure logic, the cut
between entities, the abyss, between mountains, or itself one of them,
as if something of the one or the other could be
                                        the one
From the third direction I come toward you; the impossible . . .

I am the song thrush in the currant thicket after the rain
Then we make love   When I wash myself
I play Mozart, a flute concerto, on the
                        blaring tourist radio
Mozart is also a thrush, I say   Yes, you say, and I hear
the resonant relationships between people, the brain's
value centers, the invasion of emotions, in the rhythms of amplification
of the logical maps; what I once saw as my interior ocean,
agitated, gray, when I thought I would go mad,
all these rhythms, when feedback has gone out of control, and no memory,
no dancing arabesque on the flute, in the throat of the thrush, in our
common ear, can console
Above the dry sea something like a cushion of living water . . .

when the feeling of hollowness is gone, then one can be
completely convinced: then the hollowness is
real . . .   As if we all did not
partake of this form   The whole concept
of a world of ideas, independent of us, that we did not give birth to, is
an absurdity, which leads to eternal punishment, in the underworld
                                        of paradoxes . . .

And still we construct form; are constructed of form
I listen to music   It pre-forms,
it constructs in delight, the mathematics of time,
in the perfect weighings of emotional timbres,
in a possible harmony, as actual dance . . .
The music of logical paradoxes is played in *Parmenides*,
                                as if with a strange, despairing
                                                smile . . .

V

Once again
the sea shall leap up, from the highest point   Where
we imagine the limit to be, precisely where we tran-
scend   The sea roars below the cliffs; the diabase veins
protrude like spines   We are their
rhythms, also, in the greater rhythmic system; in our
provisional attempt at counterpoint
I, too, play the second voice; in colors;
in transformations; also in the transformations of fear
The sea of fear and the sea of joy; identical; in the play of light
of valuations, beneath wandering clouds, their
shadows, lightning, oblique downpours
I walk into the wind; its pressure against my face
See the islands, the heights, the rocks   The city,
in the upper corner of the bay, shrouded in smoke
I was also part of its chemistry; when I was defined

The transformations just go on
The islands of poverty and social decay
need not be embedded
in some overriding imperial or economic structure,
I understood, yesterday, since long ago   Refugees come
wearing their veils, their darkness, their colors
We are part of this transformation, we act, the trans-
mutations in what is humanity will
go on; then we will pay the price;
or else everything is already worthless, gold . . .

If song will again be possible is not for us to decide—

VI

Out of the immeasurable set of events,
the growing number of people, jum-
bled, in confusion, sometimes united
Order is built out of syntactic fragments, not from
a prefabricated grammar; the grammar is always
secondary, in relation to meaning, where
microsyntax is forged, perpetually anew . . .   In music
proportions accumulate, in whirling numeric relations,
nor do they become visible, until
afterwards, stochastically, out of the quantity of signals . . .
We are *that* language; also *that* music, in its third coming
Then we, too, go into the ordered night

We walk in the dark sound, the wake of the turning
Then it is we who are the song; entirely possible

Music answers   As when an unknown
ability also unfolds in my left hand
We listen to be consoled   The world freed of people
feels less lonely   But we touch one another
This was the day the blackcap came up to the house   We were
making love   Then you read *Die Vernichtung*
der Juden Lettlands   This con-
fusion, recombination, now happens to us all, as in a
                                        larger brain . . .
And Mozart? I listened to Nielsen, Bach . . .
The car drives quickly through the landscape, part of a raging
                                        metabolism
Nothing is as if already completed   I hear you
showering   With the squeegee you wipe down the walls
All this is in violent construction; in its continuous
                                        destruction
But nothing is repetition; not even in pure logic

The stars come out in the pale-green luminous sky
above the dark trees   The stream rushes more quickly
It is hard to give yourself over to darkness; still
we must do it   Late in the night I move around
in the dark house   My dreams are unsettling,
filled with mockery, persecution, plans
that come to nothing   In the morning I play

Mozart, a late quartet in D major, a soft recording
on old instruments, harmonious   How
can I invoke a new change in the world?
Which leaves, which crystals, will vibrate?
I read that now one can apply
a thin diamond film to different
objects, and that human tissue does not
perceive this matter as foreign—
Only if I touch do I dare let myself be touched

The arrogance, the hubris, the blindings
in high politics, not just
inside me . . .   As if I
had the right to accuse, to judge . . .
I have seen: The judgment was all-encompassing, circular, a
sphere, in I-don't-know-how-many dimensions
transfinite, monstrous; nor do I know
what it will be used for   The
odious is all-encompassing, in civil wars, in
the hate of what is foreign, even if it is only
infinitesimal, a tiny linguistic shift . . .

I participate in conversations, virtually, or
as now in the morning, in reality, confused
About the developing political elites in Europe,
their motives, social base, recruitment,
characteristics, the differences in Denmark, Sweden . . .

What do I really know about this   What we see is
appearance, a mask   I do not like what I see

Which are the real vectors   Toward the hegemony of which resultant?
I don't accept hegemony; nor any ruler, not even
virtual   Why do I speak, why sing then of a crown, of the royal
principle, as if I were another Hölderlin   As if hierarchy
had real significance, outside the soul   Who are
die Kenner und Liebhaber? In the royal principle without hierarchy
Where we can only be among the most poor   In which
rhetorical trope? But we are in the real   On television
yesterday two small children who had been shot lay, like bloody dolls, on a bench,
pictures from Sarajevo   In the fight for some kind of hegemony;
we still don't know what kind   In the return of the principles
Then I, too, want to be a man without principles   Without first,
without second or third   Only in that way will song become possible

VII

The big sound carries its form   It carries *us;*
no matter whether life or death
I set forth over dark water, very much afraid

An invocation, of what? With our awkward symbols
we cannot know beforehand
And yet we converge there, as in the focus of a burning glass
Even voices are fused there;

including the free ones, mobile   In organum, sounding toward
who-knows-what kind of heaven
New voices, amassed in camps, emaciated
again, again, only dare speak their muteness;
here, too, are those who advocate such coercion
Every kind of coercive music is repulsive . . .

A landscape is rapidly transformed;
I already see it before my own eyes
The life of this planet, as if already spent
In the forest at night I look up
at the unyielding stars, their immovable
distances in ultra-rapid movement   A
passing satellite measures only our limitations
The stars of nations, soon exhausted,
define themselves in blood, in inhuman cruelty
As if the concentration camp itself were the emblem
of the human; in our perpetuated negation
Where we serve the hypostases of nothing
Criticism of the nation is no defense for the empire
In what timbres are we born now? In which stage?

I approach you, with something like a
chalice glistening in my hand; I walk across
infinite distance, the plains clear as glass
When we meet I will give you the chalice
Then it is a kind of death, even if
given in love   You arrived; I thought it was a dream

The chalice made of dark matter; light passes through it
in multicolored fields, gems, yellow, red, green . . .
Into the dark matter I will disappear
But still I go deeper into the labyrinth
I don't know if it is the labyrinth of the continuum
Who, what, is it that I leave to you?

The new reality, however it may be . . .
Will my tools be adequate, even if
continually made new   Which is fastest?
It depends on the power of integration   Which is also
the capacity for abstraction, and thus for simplification, fal-
                                        sification . . .
And abstraction of abstraction, in the order of infinity
In this way, too, we approach one another, even though we are
absolute magnitudes, absolute values   In the space
we continually project; or are projections of
Preserve this, these limits, the overstepping of them
Either we live in the shards of the continuum, or we are
the constructs integrated from its smallest parts . . .
Or we exist only there, in the continuum of zero; where the labyrinth ceases

VIII

I want to be in what is . . .
also in what is luminous, resonant oblivion
The branches of one part of the birch tree now have yellow leaves

The smell of autumn, the feel of autumn air, harsh, slightly bitter
I will listen to all the masses for the dead, not heard
in times to come, while the images that come from social television
stack up the corpses, already almost dry, leaf upon leaf
of alternative, virtual universes   This is not where we are
Death is real; but it's not the sole reality
I will also listen to a new German requiem   In which
I already hear a new disaster, like a low, muffled tone
Deepest in there is no solution   Nor farthest out
The extremes forms take make them plain   Each form a falsification
What is is incomprehensible, comprehensible, nameless, possessed of all names,
visible it is invisible, invisible it is visible, unheard
I listen to it   Present it is absent, absent
it is present   In this excluded third term we are included;
what cannot exist we encompass, as the single most significant thing
In the cracks it is whole   In the whole it is utterly fragmented
The silence sings   Nobody hears the sound   Almighty
it lacks power   Only the absence of power prevails   Dead, it lives
Living, it is dead   Only what is is not
I touch your flesh . . .

IX

Sparks, slow fire   That color, glowing
molten glass   But not amorphous   Not
fluid; another kind of form   Not crystal
either   Living form! Where cell is connected to cell

morphogenetically   Immediately contiguous; then also
                              in the brain
in increasingly complex additional connections
The burning bush; glowing forth—
While the pillars of clouds, the pillars of fire travel
                            the horizon
Only if we answer can form arise
Now I see the image of a face approaching
                   in these colors
shifting, already through the whole spectrum,
then also through the colors of death, black, white
The image of a ship comes, the
               back of a running animal, a
wall painting, from some book   Leaf
upon leaf   Sign against sign;
but we are in this continuousness . . .

Can unity with
the incomprehensible exist for me too? The
inconceivable, with no image, no concept,
and thus beyond all form . . .
What shows itself to me with no image?

  X

Time has *its* instrumentarium   But we
pass through it   As if we passed

through all the interstices among notes
Things look at us, quietly vibrating
All things tremble, in fear or in joy;
or in a cry of pain, its penetrating sound
Your rose looks at me now; the one you gave me
Never will it vanish in the rushing of time—

How can I widen the interplay of strata, surfaces, networks,

                                          spaces

or multi-dimensional objects
Fractal lightning   O blind, standing wave
Rising like the heart; an arrow,

                        or a flood

There is a path straight through the hand held upright,
through its cracks, its earth, into
Hell in its radiance, its splendor
There we are demonic angels
before the terrified Mary
The punishment is ours
in that we punish others

XI

Devaluation   Out of this comes the sound of phantasmagoric

                                          music   In

sounds of destruction, in strict imitation, in free

counterpoint, to death, to life   As if they were
the same universal point   The singularity, where everything
                                        gathers
How shall a new lightness be born? In its perfection
We are chosen, stochastically; then become irretrievable, before
                                        annihilation comes
As if every selection were natural, in God's tree—

the actual movements of world economies beneath a membrane clear as glass:
We are defined there, starting from each person's
particular infinity   Then we are reduced,
infinitely; toward poverty first, then
death   For their consolation   We hear
the grotesque music   All
of history sounds, in its simultaneity,
enormous, impossible to perceive
even in the ear's moment of death; the ear that sees—

There is no way to escape
Even as infinitesimal increments
we carry the projected function . . .
as if it were our own father, or mother
                        on our back
up out of Hell, burning, crystal clear—

The sea of finance capital, of over 7 trillion dollars,
moving freely over the surface of the globe, without
limits, without controls, and with the power

to crush nations . . .   Literally
controlled by no one, in electronic
arteries, in capillaries, where nothing
breaks down   Electronic gold has no colors
The shadow follows us   The rudder is of diamond

XII

Where I am going
you do not follow   But I will
think of you, there,
wherever I am, and where you
are, along with our child
Then I will be there

XIII

I prepare myself for language's breaking out
into a larger space   To a more complete music
That's what I imagine! But I can never know in
advance   I only know that I cannot turn
                              back,
that I cannot look back   Recursive
functions are something else; every re-
                              entry
occurs in the future   Participates, thus, in oblivion—

The changes are chemical   We must say
no to false images; or
evil will multiply   We must also be able to look
evil in the eye: Gorgonian counterpoint
Ourselves partly evil   For nothing is
pure; not even pure logic
The syllogisms of shit stitch, like a sewing machine   I see
the spruces, shining dark green under the snow

We are neither too late nor too early;
an irremediable aspect of time   Everything
else is nostalgia, in either direction
Thus the Gospel is in the needlepoint of the eye
with its infinity of angels
with wings that are dark or light . . .

All this is easy to say   Last night I dreamed
about my fear, something to do with
Jewish graves that were desecrated   Nelly Sachs's
delusions were wholly realistic   Dirt-red,
the color of hell, is here too   Not
the hell we shall build up with law, from below . . .

XIV

A big white car is parked on the asphalt path
between the houses   You can see it through the gray, brown, and white
branches of the trees   A car like that could be used to escape,
I think to myself   As if the war were already here   Which is
not the case   The war in Europe is still localized
in limited hotbeds   Pus shining white, or
some other image   Why do people die? Civil
wars on ethnic or religious grounds, rising up out of the
past? I don't know   All matter is memory   What I see are
remains of Stalinistic communism fused with
currents of fascism, old and new   As if this
alliance were not very old, under the skin of politics
What is a nation? What is Swedishness? As if these
questions themselves had led to murder   The territorial instinct, the earth
out of which one is born, perhaps the earth of the grave, the earth of one's
father and mother; *dulce et decorum est pro patria mori,*
no, dammit! I saw pictures from Ravensbrück, and from
other camps   The same sorts of faces as those from Bosnia and Somalia
The faces of suffering and starvation   Are all images
executioners' images? No! But every image is utterly excluded
Living things, agents of the invisible god, they are
                                             not images
Once I believed images were our children; but that's not
                                             true either
Every child has its own perfect face   In whatever
                         transformation of suffering or joy

it may find itself   Every face is of earth   We are the one earth
Our pact with the murderers, how does it look? Faces

turned away; earth averted

XV

only if I dare to go deeper
What is deeper?
That I can find out only
by going deeper
The answer to Pilate's question

Worry for myself is mixed
with worry for our child
maybe also with worry for you
Our souls flutter
Our brains have butterfly brilliance
The stars look at us, with their distant light,
their giddiness, in their nests of nothing

We cannot surrender to any totality other
than the unimaginable, without dying
This the sole totality we can take in

XVI

I heard your voice
say goodnight to me
when you didn't think
I could hear you
It was naked, without
reservation   Then you
woke me, utterly,
so much that I
couldn't sleep
I was elated

XVII

Every word carries
all its despair
all its joy
We carry one another

XVIII

Last night I saw
the point central to
the underground man's neurosis:
Freedom's point   Every

action, every insight, bad or good
foolish or wise
hinges on this one point
All acts of humiliation, internal or external,
and all crimes against others
are set in motion
when this point is denied or refused
The point takes flight, flees
Like a bird
It has its own will, its bird-logic
I've known this for a long time
Freedom also has the potential to annihilate
because it is limitless
in each person
Nor is there anything
that cannot become a prison
But a prison
can never fly like a bird

I hear the motion of breath in the beating of wings

XIX

Freezing fog drifts between the naked trees
a woodpecker gleams red, a black thrush
You talk to your sister on the phone, as you usually do
on Saturday morning   Peace should exist

Society is undergoing disintegration, ideologically,
humanly, economically   The historic compromise
between the working class and the bourgeoisie no longer exists,
destroyed by an arrogant right, and met by a startled
still sleeping working class that will be divided,
its less serviceable parts marginalized   This is
the basic sketch for the perpetuation of a new civil war
What is happening is hard to describe, hard to get a handle on
hard to understand for me as well as for others   Why
should I of all people understand better? I see despair dawning
in those who believed themselves secure in their lives
but who now face unemployment, just as
social safety nets threaten to disappear   Economic
reasons are cited; in a system of consciously constructed pseudo-explanations
Even most of its proponents believe in them, hold them
as true   Every civil war builds on illusions and fear
Even war between individuals; whatever bonds may exist between them

To recapitulate images from history: After the first
world war, exhaustion, victory, inability to
build a new order, growing dissolution, chaos   Re-
vanchism   Economic depression   Then the waiting
for Germany, the generalized war initiated by Germany
This dread waiting, 1938, 1939   When I was conceived
After the cold war another period of exhaustion, an-
other victory   Perhaps we are in the presence of generalized
civil war, internal division, hatred   Should we prefer
the empire? As Dante did? Or Ezra Pound, Heidegger   Or

for that matter Brecht? We love dissolution and chaos passionately,
I hear a voice say, I know whose   It is not here that I shall say it
It is not easy   There are no nations   Pillars of fire precede
the returning, in human terms, lost son

XX

It will soon be March 1993; late in the century; what
we think of as turning points often are not, or are
turns toward something entirely different   Theories
cross one another, as in a civil war
I hear someone in Sarajevo deny it is
a civil war; for him it is rather
a desperate defense, of Europe, of the
possibility of a multinational culture   I look out
through the birch trees' branches   Snow on the ground, less here
than in Bosnia   Here, where everything
still functions   Does it? What is Europe? Does this country belong
there? Here or there! We stand before the same fundamental
challenges   Am I capable of answering? Is Serbia the kingdom of Castile
annihilating Granada?
Immigration; the media's version of world revolution; the fall
of liberal thought, together with communism?
Emigration; religious orthodoxy, instead of
justice   Dike's vision is utterly blind   Nothing
hangs in the balance   Hypostatized nothing is
heavy as a centner; in one of the old systems of measure   What

do we measure? We approach liminal values
without having the exact measure   Soon our cup runs over
Trees die; humans die; people, our kinfolk die
Bonds go straight through nations   The judgment on
us all, maybe that too will die in the end   We are
synchronically defined; maybe time also has roots,
like invisible dimensions, with the same kind of limits
simple time has, simple space   Then
we move alongside them; centuries or millennia
have never had any significance whatsoever;
except for us, arbitrary measures, in our love
in our pain and in our despair, like an ocean

XXI

The words moved out into the darkness
hovered like butterflies
somehow freestanding
I heard the abyss breathing

XXII

The verdure is very green   For the night,
when there would be frost, you put white gauze
over the little apple tree, which stood there

in the white dawn, like a ghost, in a wedding
                                        gown, womanly,
or like the lady who lost her head, you said . . .

Even the foliage crystallizes   In 1915 Klee wrote
in his journal about what the war did to him
I crystal   About his heart as an abstraction
About Mozart, who saved himself by crossing over, without forgetting
his Inferno   I, too, was there in that crossing

XXIII

We cross the river of light; its whirling kernels
                                        of darkness
We cross the river of darkness; to what? No one knows

Night's strings move upward,
irradiated, toward the extinguished stars
Out of which sonorous day? We'll soon reach the apex
of light, one more time in order
One time will be the last   We delve into, we construct
the brain of Hell   The order is the same

Music streams from the ground of being, from becoming
from the moment of silence between them,
to exaiphnes, of which resonant words and their
derivative silence are also a part . . .

Meanings are superimposed, as are meanings of silences
if we can now speak of more than a single one . . .
What is being blocked out   What is in us
                                    as a high-pitched tone? The
                        cricket-like sounds come closer, come to be

XXIV

Each time we get a bit older; but we are
still in our childishness   Human lives all around me, I see them
in their helplessness; wonder what it is I'm not seeing,
which resources, which transcendings   For we are
in no way bound; except as parts of the stochastic, no
less real for that   Catatonic powers are moving
Inside there, in the shimmering chambers, maybe the new life is
                                    born, unavoidably . . .
That is not what I believe   We are in the crystal chambers

We shall crush history, its unendurable crystal, which is
without deceit; deceit resides within us, almost exclusively

Already the verdure pales at the apex of sunlight
Now it is lit again, sparkling with sun   We are
exposed; the possibilities of catastrophes play
In us lies the entire potential   The whole brain of Hell;
the canonical Paradise   We look to one another; one another'
s monsters of light, one another's cures that bring darkness—

The apex of light   In just that bre-
ath of turning   And back again
The unheard-of, the immense moves, in its permanence

XXV

Bengt Anderson

We are in the deepening architecture, its folds of light, its
construction and destruction   Fold is laid against fold
We are *polytropoi anthropoi*, people of
                        many turnings; our journey takes us
in all directions; even those that do not exist   Summers
connect to this summer   This summer may be your last   I said:
When you're buried six feet deep, you'll eat no more
                        chicken meat!
I see the earth's folds; the earth is also of light, earth-light
You'd been given two units of blood; which made your brain live
We spoke about music: Gubaidulina, Couperin, Bach   About a circle
of friends who knew one another, who inspired one another
Yesterday I thought: The language of Heraclitus is untranslatable;
the language of Parmenides is universal   Consequently: God, or death
The same language, at the same time   The folds of the irreconcilable, shining

XXVI

The unending line of the landscape, through time, through laws,
their alteration, through wars, through our indifference   What is, for
us, nearest and best? The spikes of the grasses move in the wind   Images
at the limit of what is unendurable; we are spoon-fed, or beak-
fed, like the baby crow here, insatiable   The flock of starlings flies
I look northeastward, up toward the crest of the ridge, the beech forest above
the sloping fields   Where the birds came; every year they are fewer
When we break through the laws, we do so under intolerable duress;
or in the tedium and desperation of indifference   Dry, on the surface
What we break through each time has at least three dimensions   On
the other side of the ridge the primary rock drops straight down to the sea, red gneiss
with black diabase passages   In the west, Cambrian sandstone slabs, gray,
with fossil traces, emerge under layers of earth close by the sea—

The rock keeps breaking down   We stand near the fault-cliffs
We who are human have not been here long   Under the sun
Late into the night the moon shone yellow-red over Kullaberg; the sea
out there, distant, in its breathing   I touched
                            the water with my fingers
The wild roses still blooming, their colors   Still June, its light

The land in its majesty   The fatherland's angels, archi-
tectonic light-forms, move over land and sea, where
the land ends   The sun and moon move   The wind moves, the ex-
tinguished stars   You are in the field picking strawberries, which we'll
eat later with sugar and yogurt, sheltered from the wind   At night the sea

was gray, the rock gray, barely visible, the moon invisible in the gray
If we are translations, in the dynamic world of signs, forever
strange, who will read us? There will be no fatherland, nor any
revolt, our movements awkward, *amechanos*, the wings, our own and others',

slash us till we bleed—

XXVII

Which laws do we break, break
through? Which law of value, which accumulation
of humanity? What is repulsive in the world increases
The abyss is also *here*, oil of genocide
on our hands, in our society, innocent only in its
sloth, old guilt repressed, new guilt unacknowledged
Here, too, Dionysus returns, with his
train of dancing stars   The Queen of the Night,
blazing with stars, has also come   Flutes   Stringed
instruments   There are people here who, like Ismene,
believe they are choosing life   They deny the existence of
guilt, of binding justice   Themis's, Dike's,
even the laws of the state; subterranean or heavenly;
even the way of due measure, of *metron*   For in
reality we are immoderate   Shrill was the sound of our climb
up the slope, up out of the abyss   Down there is the sea
Today, in the storm and the rain, the sound comes from the north
lower-pitched than the soughing of the forest, gusts of wind rattling the house

Who? Who is it we shall bury   Who shall bury us
I watch graves being dug in the hard, stony soil
The bodies are laid down quickly   It will happen here, too, when
cold-storage rooms stop working, when the undertakers
no longer have the means for their current procedures   Then
the dead won't need to wait   They'll see justice done   No one
stands outside things as they are   Whosoever believes he
does cannot describe them either, except without contra-
dictions   In the realm of the dead   Or the kingdom of heaven   I see Gödel's
shy, gray smile   Who
does not want to be among the living   In heaven   On earth
The flower I pick is called restharrow, deep pink, with white wings
flying out of its lips at an angle from the center
I put it in the little vase with the pale pink rose

XXVIII

The sea was visible in the distance; through the gray a white
stripe of death-surf breaking on the shore   We descend
in the underworld of the fugue; together   The sound of the Battle Song-
Threnos   Gorgonian; the work of Pallas Athana; the first
polyphony,
if we can believe Pindar   We don't feel the necessity
of grace
Reeds and metal instruments play   Before us
the Mozart labyrinth—

In the destruction of which sort of brain
shall we live . . .   For we are in its pathways,
their deterioration, their unexpected geneses
Polyphony can also be born
of petrifaction   New laws
come, thrusting up out of the earth
We are always coming back from Hades . . .
The dance rises like a rainbow out of the earth—
But we're pried open, as with a can opener

How am I to exist in this shattered
human language   That is in its
continuum, we just don't know which one   And I,
detached from this as I am,
in my local inhumanity   Who
observes us   Who scrutinizes us?
The dark eyes look at us out of their darkness
How we treat one another   Live with one another

Conditions under which all language ceases
But that is not where *we* are   We can
still speak to one another, converse, we are not
yet song   What are we singing?
Again and again comes the question   We are
creatures who ask questions   The song alone does not sing

I learned something   What have I given in return?
What can I give now, from this distance   The sound tran-
scends everything; every phoneme is decisive   We are not permitted
to fail   Here, too, the resounding clash of nature's weapons   By the sea,
in the evening, on the road out to the Iron Age cairns of gray rubble,
the Tear Mounds, I heard the curlew, its cry   It flew
straight out to sea, its beak shone in the sun   Even at the tip of the point
the sandstone slabs extend into the sea   I touched the clear
                                                            water;
knew it to be the water of death   She who walked by my side said:
For the first time this summer we're at one
Somewhat later: For the first time your step is light
Now I hear the long, gray fugue growing, as if it were coming out of the sea
                                                            as if it were
one single brain   Also out of internal persecution, internal af-
                                                            fliction

I look at the primary rock, the sandstone, the earth   The birds
The plants   Listen to the birds   At twilight a thrush sang
or a starling, hard to say which, for I had never heard
such phrases before, except maybe in Charlie Parker and Eric Dolphy
Beautiful, clear as water, but also half suffocated, twisted   It was probably
a thrush   It's Bengt, I thought, he died in the night   Yesterday he phoned
to tell us not to come   He didn't have the strength   He'd only managed
to get out of bed for 30 minutes   His voice rapidly grows weaker

XXIX

The way out of sorrow, when
resistance becomes inevitable   And the sign of battle
appears in the heavens; when all bonds break
in defense of what ultimately remains, where defense is
impossible   I thought it was possible to wait,
to wait out the change, but I see it is not
How do I fail those still alive? A conversation with the dead
goes on; takes almost all my time; and a conversation
with myself, as if *I* were already dead? I don't know
Sometimes I don't know if I'm dead or alive
Inquisition is not conversation   I will not bow down
                                    to any kind of logic;
nor to the destruction of logic . . .

The lines of the landscape close   I take my bearings
from points of home, accidental, abandoned
also by the future; from the impossible   I see
points of birth, points of death   Sutures
burst open, close up again   On this day fog came from the sea
Contours of the trees, dark; brown horses in the meadow
The torches of the dark mullein glow yellow, purple   The bedstraw also
glows yellow, over the grass's various shades of green, brown

Three times I have touched the sea, its hardness   I grew up
by its basin, later on I moved away   I am
in many realms, one after the other, simultaneously   They make the sounds of

the snakes' heads   I played the flute here once, *one* time, through
the window, over the landscape, out toward the sea   That was
enough; just a few notes, a few arabesques   Soon
we will leave here, never to return   The dead woman in the house
is finally dead now, you say, as we prepare to go   There's no
harmony here; we shall live through this as well   In its
diversification, its various misunderstandings, its burning
pain   Shadows of abandonment came, came and went   We
are those who bear this life, until someone else takes over   The mullein's dark
torches also in Hades; or the greater realm of death where

everyone is at home

Now I'll place a call to Hades; if my friend is not dead
I'll tell him about the crane you saw at the mouth of the stream, the Fylle—
All the other birds are there too, and the frogs, in Children's Hades . . .

XXX

We spoke of death   And of God   Someone had asked you
if you shouldn't think about what was to come
Then you rose in revolt   If I meet God, you said, in precisely
the moment before death, I'll have something to tell him
that will blast him through billions of years   In any case
something like that; I can't remember the exact words   Saw your
head, its face, with the same expression as when you once
listened to the music   And I saw its presence in you   I spoke
of hope, that we did not know, that nowadays cancer
more and more often was curable   I saw that you no longer

believed this   Together we listened to language resounding, its
music   Then you grew tired   Complained that your tongue
was partially paralyzed   I'm going out, I said   Walked to the edge of the cliff,
toward Aspen, gray, the lake Rilke also looked out over,
most likely, when he completed *Orpheus. Eurydike. Hermes*   We
walked there last fall, together; I could see you were
very ill; though back then I thought it was your heart   Thought
you would not live another year   Now one and a half months remain

You can still manage   Intuitions of death come; they are part
of life   On top of the cliff, among autumn leaves, velvet boletes grew, their
stems shimmering red   This summer, alone, I bowed my head to the water
Before I returned, from death, to you who are still alive
Suddenly you were exhausted; Kerstin and I left, drove
back to the sea, beyond the limit of the fault line   I felt great joy
My wish: that you'll die at your lake, by your cliff, at the utmost
verge of your music, for it is your own   Even the music you did not write
No one can take that from you   Its sound is in rebirth

XXXI

I hear my father's laughter, its brightness, I see his smile   Sovereign
When he wards off the spite, the snide irony he lived through
at the kitchen table in Färgaryd   And learned to defend against, with a mechanism
that would not jam   Or so I believe   For I was not old enough
to understand my father   Except for what I saw in the figure of the man
Now he smiles in Hades   As if all of us were the dreams of shades

But if the brain only grows from the point of the impossible . . .   Beyond
all natural selections   We are coal from strange stars,
older than the sun that lights us, and which in turn
will go out, or rapidly be destroyed   We are cosmogenetic
beings   Creatures of a day   One, or not one   Dream-shadows
We are members of the order Projection   Pitched against

the sky of the impossible

When someone tries to take my
sovereignty from me, my right to be free   Then rebellion comes
of its own accord, with regard for no one, completely beyond my control
The darkness, Apollonian, resounds; even in the

light that stills pain . . .

Nor shall you deprive me of my death!

How do I enter the labyrinth of error . . .   Again and again
Fallacious music sounds as well   Is a part of
life; constantly full of error   In the striving toward universality
there is also error; for there is no perfect
foundation; not even the eye of a needle's point . . .
The only thing that exists in that case is mercy!

We seek out the necessary silence, to be
able to live   There, where it finds us   Like
death, or a stage preceding death, still
revocable   I write you, old friend,

about death   About music's utter complexity
in the face of it; and the enormous courage that exists within it
Which you always possessed through all the years   I am weeping
Straight through your despairing frightened voice I hear
it   The music is pain objectified   We are parts of it
The silence smiles   As if even the pain were Mozart; dark, silent

XXXII

You're fighting with lions, I said to you, in the conversation
where it seemed you had come back from the dead
I thought we had talked to each other for the last time   Maj
had just told me that mostly you slept, or
were in your youth, your mind partly confused   Your voice
was weak at first; then it came back in all its sonority
There's something very difficult, I can't really manage it, you said
You couldn't explain it; but I think it has something to do with
death, what it is, or with God, as you understand him, half
non-existent   It is part of your agony   With this we do battle

The movement in all directions at once   It integrates
Disintegrates   Pain   Pleasure   Grace-Constraint
But to try to be part of this without too much fear
We enter in   Tonalities are projected, their low
pitches   Gravitation   But we move toward the abyss of pain, toward
the invisible   What, whom, do we meet there? In which coming—

We enter into the infinite brain . . .   The plain is
endless   Mountains, seas, humans: accidental
The last bear all the significance   We shall remain with them
Whoever they are; whoever we are; independent of whichever world

What holds us together? Only the impossible vision?
But we have never been able to know what is possible
We move hyperrealistically in social life   Ourselves
mobile within ourselves   Taking stands continually
Every break in the continuum a leap   Every leap a blinding
We spring from lightworld to lightworld   In our blinding darkness
We can do nothing else   As if all of us existed only in the bondage of the will
From inside each autonomy grows the light of grace; when it is not murderous;
as if the Graces existed, were alive, in their ambiguity, their infinite
                                        delicacy . . .

XXXIII

I sent you the music of pain, on tape, so that you
would be able to listen to it, in the time left to you   But
it was too late   You can't take it
You can still take in shreds of music   Dowland is
played for you, among what you most loved   To this
you can still respond   Maj asks if you
recognize Dowland, know who it is, and you answer
yes   As if this were the last communication between

the two of you   Once, entirely on your own, you read
Schoenberg's *Harmonielehre*, yourself tried, untrained, to write
twelve-tone music, but later destroyed what you'd done   Failed
to pursue it   Twice, that I know of, you tried
to take your own life   That was before you met Maj   You are now
yourself in the ultimate music, yourself pain   Confusion and
dreams   What you say follows dream logic
I believe that inside you, within the destruction of your body, harmony
still exists   As if it too were part of pain

I imagine that you wake to the confusion of dreams
Fragments of life, whirling, in new permutations
I remember your using that word, 36 years ago, when you
spoke of the music you wanted to write, that I did not
                                    really know
you were actually trying to write   We spoke about Schoenberg
You showed me music by Satie, Messiaen, the conceptions
implicit in the scores   Mostly we talked about jazz
You wrote arrangements for the band we both played in,
combinatorics was in this, too; as was confusion, for
there is no difference   What you are living now is also life
I wouldn't be surprised if your voice suddenly were there
on the telephone   As if a new permutation arose   In the
                                   infinite series . . .

XXXIV

We are falling through the abyss   Voices, of terror,
come to me   I try to answer but sense
my awkwardness, my lack of analysis and also of empathy . . .
I talk about righteousness confronting righteousness,
that both lack mercy; mercy must come equally from both sides
Then I feel the emptiness of my words   But I can't
accept the hatred of nation for nation, not even in its inverse,
                                        self-sacrificing form . . .
I can hear the despair is genuine   Wonder at my own coldness
Soon it will be Yom Kippur   Would Kol Nidre hold for me as well?

The degradation of human lives in big cities . . .   At the same time
a new recombination occurs, in a new *Ars magna*
We are part of this great art   We have
                        no control over it   I see
faces everywhere, in their completeness, also
in people reduced almost to nothing, destitute
                        Where shall we find a new image?
A form seeks us out   We will be completely unprepared
Madness everywhere   Also inside my self

Everything's one single stammering   Expression that went wrong,
got stuck, in disconsolate deadlocks, cramps
I see that rage is no way out, as it is for Adam
Michnik; in any case it is not my way   We'll play
the shit out of them, Bengt   At every point there's expression

Even in the uttermost tenderness; in the outermost darkness
Schoenberg's last word was: *Harmonie!* That is where music is—
in its transfiguration of pain, in its playfulness, its lofty lightness

XXXV

A new wind blows through the world   Democracy is power
I hear someone say, from Moscow, a former
advisor to Gorbachev, now a supporter of Yeltsin's
unconstitutional ukase to dissolve the parliament
and carry out new elections in December under another
as yet not entirely drafted constitution   Maybe this *is*
a democratic coup; in any event its opponents are
probably worse   Outside the parliament building
last night old Communists set up barricades   The whole lot
surrounded by Interior Ministry troops   The parliament has deposed
Yeltsin and sworn in Rutskoi as president   A
civil war is entirely possible   According to Sky News
this morning Moscow goes back to work as usual

Within what sort of anxiety are we enclosed   I see us
on bridges, windblown organic strings, shooting out
over the abyss   Toward what we never know; will never know
There is no security   I quote Hölderlin, on
that which saves   But say nothing about the god's presence,
terrifying   We cross the water to get home from the island   Autumn, blue-gray
twilight clouds from the low pressure area south of us   The trees stand luminous

Warships in the gloaming: autumn maneuvers called "Hurricane"
The moon looms   We drive toward the city   You say:
even in the middle of Stockholm, Sweden's a sparsely populated country
On the island conversation was possible   And music   We picked
                                        trumpet chanterelles
The islands rest in their world of water   I cannot count them   We in-
habit this inalienable language   Each splinter of which bears its worth
In a symphony by Revueltas I recognized a phrase of Gershwin
T nods in acknowledgment   I did not know Revueltas's work
I talk about Panufnik, his composition *Arbor Cosmica*,
say that I hardly believed Panufnik existed, back when T talked
about him, 20 years ago   We stand in astonishment before each other
Then I talk about curves that explode exponentially,
quantities of people, exploding scientific knowledge, ex-
ploding art   Beneath us we feel the security of the islands
We are this explosion   Cosmopolitan cities grow

Different kinds of agony   I know you are dying,
Bengt; perhaps you are already dead; all day yesterday,
my birthday, was a waiting for the telephone call
That did not come   Then reports of fighting in Moscow
A red-brown uprising, soldiers and demonstrators,
with the Russian fascist leader at the head, he spoke of revolution,
stormed the city hall, and later the TV building   Now, this
morning, the parliament building is attacked by soldiers and
tanks   Rifle and cannon fire   It's all a matter of time
before the revolt is stifled, in Moscow   In Russia nothing is settled
I listen to Giacinto Scelsi's 4th string quartet, play it for

you, Bengt, in *your* agony   There are different kinds of battles with death
Different kinds of battles for life   I remember when we talked about
the 5th string quartet, a requiem for Michaux   Remember
when we, 35 years ago, talked about Michaux's phrase: *re-*
duced to humility by disaster   You showed it to me, it
has followed me ever since   Now you inhabit your disaster   In your daughter's
voice, in her tone, I heard you may no longer be anxious
That you smiled, when regards from close friends were
                                                given to you
Now I return to the picture on TV   Almost all the time CNN broadcasts
live   What is still alive   I want to believe that you are still living
I will play for you what will become your requiem   I will
                                                light candles

XXXVI

There are moments when music becomes clear
even in its utmost complexity, unknown
even at the point of simplicity, the needle's point of nothing

There the last music becomes the first
Nothing is cancelled out   We are at the great divide
Where we touch one another, in real integrity

The battle is over   You fought to the last
against death   Your last words may have been, "This is shit!"
when the phlegm kept you from breathing   In the end

your heart could no longer hold out   Maj, Tomas, and Annika
were with you   The day before you died, a warm fall day,
Maj opened the window, the great titmice were singing   She asked
if you heard them, and you hummed yes in answer   Your last music
was Billie Holiday; the blues   After Maj phoned last night
I lit candles and played Mozart's string quintet in G minor,
the Budapest Quartet, an old recording in mono
Kerstin and I sat together, silent, listening
Then I put out the lights   Now you are in the highest music

XXXVII

To the world as it returns, in its individuality . . .
We are light of the light   The gray silence in November, the
placid trees, lashes of the whip in other people's faces, imper-
fection in the life of substances, where we all exist, vir-
tually, in contemporaneous alternative worlds, if time has any place in
this vision, in this light of light, where we all see one another . . .
In Dis, the city of Hell, all these worlds moved, in one continuous
                                                    din . . .
Mozart was not there; I played music, thought: now I'll see
                                                    to the living . . .

I give myself over to the greater memory, to the interior,
where all substances exist, actual or virtual,
in greater or lesser degrees of perfection . . .

The spectral forms move   Whether in Plato's heaven
or hell makes no difference either   We are
the real shadows made from the light of shadows, from
the folds of genocide, the surfaces of pain, the lives of the exploited
For they are the living, not the dead   This
Allhallows Eve I will also light candles for those still living . . .

Remember now how I was struck, as if receiving a vision
when I heard, or read, that at the head of Bach's bed
after his death someone found a copy of Leibniz's
De arte combinatoria   I've discovered the note
among my papers, but with no indication of its source   So I can
not verify this, have searched long in vain   Maybe this is
just another of those legends surrounding all such deathbeds
This does not prevent its bearing an internal truth
All of us live in the great brain, damaged or undamaged

XXXVIII

Slowly Hades retreats   This time
The transparent sea touches the shore
The edge of fine sand shifts, softly, exactly

XXXIX

Snow fell upon the darkness   Upon the two
who walked up Allhallows Hill in Lund
in December, 1958   He didn't believe it was true
Nor was it, except for
a moment, outside of time   The world
closed its huge eye, whose inside was blinding stars
Then sleep came and pain   The world is strange
The world is a strange, an alien place   So-
cieties are warped, shot apart   Nothing
can be predicted   The future is the surging
of other waves on the seashore   Winter

I am still seeking precision   He who was I
no longer exists   Nor does she who walked beside me

And if we amputate one another's brains . . .   Instead
of helping one another grow   I see the dark
of bitterness flow like honey   The taste of it
penetrates everything   Take it all away
Everything is being created anew   At every moment
From the morning of the world   So much greater
then is the blame   What are you talking about?

We seek the order
that also embraces the mystery of creation
even if it were continuous . . .

The world's abysses open rapidly   And we stare
into them, as with the astonishment of God   Very far
away I hear the bright voice, as on a sped-up
tape, perhaps half a tone higher   What it says
moves within some other intellect   Resembling my own

All life so fragile toward death   And yet death
has no chance   Death is nothing

How shall we take care of one another? And if we don't want
to be taken care of? If we just want to die in peace?
The gray darkness grows   Still we light candles   The number of dead
also grows   Some are snatched back; a miracle that grows
As if these were sheer structures of handiwork, originating in God:
Feather-forms, leaf-forms   Dance; also in its mirror-form

XL

About that which lacks form   Diffuse power
radiating through the empire   While the distinct
forms of humans, their perfection, is destroyed, torn
apart   In reciprocal killing   How are we separated out?
Images surround us   Painted on the abstract mountains

I look inside myself   What do I see, which
kind of arrogance? We are aspects of the continuum of pain

Treachery exists; ties to genocide;
the complete absence of all structures
When you let yourself fall toward me
I will receive you, all the same, with what I have
or do not have   What is then born out of nothing, like
an abstract flower filled with blood, with love . . .

The protracted, low-grade genocide just goes on
and on, in Bosnia-Herzegovina   The totality of
suffering grows   Shame grows   Europe's shame   My per-
sonal shame   For no one does anything to prevent it
With this comes acceptance; a kind of gangrene in
the brain of Europe   Every individual human who is murdered
burns with an entirely clear flame   An unheard-of, a monstrous fire!

Seeing this as an aspect of empire helps almost
no one either   No part of the universe is without order
says the philosopher   But if no point exists outside the order,
we cannot know whether or not it is ordered   The tower
of dead gets new storeys   The Hubble Telescope is being repaired
Young Swedish neo-Nazis get high on *The Triumph of the Will*
The bondage of the will bears all the known aspects of God

The abstract earth moves underfoot
There are no footholds, where we fall in God's virtuality

XLI

The dark face of Dike, in the underworld   From there
justice comes, returning, from within the darkness
We stand in the sheen of the blinding knife

For a long time I've looked at the Gorgon's face,
straight into the radiant eyes   Polyphonous, the sound
of this music   With light we blind the light—

XLII

In the presence of each word is the utmost abandonment,
as if each carried its own abyss   Radiance surrounds each word
like a dark aura   Before which I bow my head

Murders occur at an ever-increasing distance
Even when they are quite close; farthest away
when we carry them out, if that's what we do
Human wings flapping afar in the darkness

But the laws of the city are never our internal laws
We observe the lower laws
even as we believe we are breaking them   We are
dark together   We touch one another, with
the tips of our shoes, in the dust   We give one another
fragments of the laws; very shiny and sharp

We will crush one another planetarily   We are not
merciful; who would show mercy?
Has goodness existed, just occasionally, its gaze
averted? Sometimes we don't know what we see
The gaze is dark; it looks off into the distance

Snow-trees   Completely still   Sun shines
through the intact formations   A string stretch-
ing to life   We don't know what we have

My voice could reach out to you, touch you
for I am no longer so afraid   Not of that!
I am inside the darknesses   Sometimes I cannot distinguish
one from another   I hear the light of your voice

1789   Mozart's music existed, widest in its span
Soon Haydn would travel to London   The
collective Mozart is an absurdity, a falsification . . .
Collective forms can remove part of
what's marginally evil, nothing more   That's a lot,
it can affect existence   Sickness, hunger,
a roof over one's head   But in cases of more intimate
degradations something else pertains   We are sexual
beings   The sound of light moves iridescently   We are
encounters between individuals, or nothing at all   We burst into pieces

There is a movement from inside and below   How
can we hold onto it   We can only hold on

as individuals   Now I touch the knife   Now I touch
the child   I see the small, dark, serious faces
as in a dream   Old-fashioned guns, with heavy barrels
Who organizes them? Or what sort of self-organization?
Crystals form around fragments of pain
The impossible child stirs   In the face of its monstrous birth
There are also other children   And other monsters
A battle is waged among humanity's parts; different kinds of
division   Different kinds of mathematics, generated or
self-generated   In which palingenesis   Which kinds of Lepidoptera,
of the night or the day, all their different colors, darkness, whiteness
The rebirth of class struggles   As if in cramp; so much deg-
radation, pain   Such enormous deformation   I feel the
white hand-wing strike my cheek   Contempt and disgust
strike, do battle with an unheard-of love   We could be
one single humanity   But even exploitation is differentiated
A tiny increment of advantage   And oppression's crystal
precipitates out   In its shimmering palace of colors   There are also
human dwelling places   Even for those with no roofs over their heads

XLIII

Anna R

The conversation that began 35 years ago
Once I literally held her fast, when she
would have lifted off into the heaven of her angst

She still has something to complete
With my fingers in her bristly hair I held her down
The universe pulsated, in all its transparency

XLIV

The fragile weave of your life's
tapestry of colors dis-
colors now, tears
apart from inside   Still
your soul is wholly
alive, flesh and blood

Two metastases in your liver, one in each
lobe, I hear you say   Yes, I say
Then there's not much more
to say, in words   And yet words come
straight through the warmth   About worth   About your words,
their significance   Which I'd always seen
Thanks, you say, and I feel a little embarrassed

There is no other person I know
who has your goodness, light as a feather,
cautious, shy as a bird   And then
your voice comes, and carries, entirely clear,
vibrating, as if it came from
the center of all existence   As if all your

angst, all your fear had blown away
This happens even now, in your dying
Your voice is wholly rooted, your warmth intact
In your presence I have never been alone

XLV

Now Kore no longer wants
to return to the earth
in the cycle of vegetation, you say

XLVI

The unknown language arises within me   How shall
I receive it? Maybe it too is death
I saw your transfigured head, resting on a pillow
when you could no longer manage to sit up   You'd tried to eat
three shrimps, you said, but couldn't manage that either
We held onto each other hard   We have always trusted each other

XLVII

What is created in a new, unfamiliar latticework of cells,
replete with transparent connections
The way our time poses questions marks but

does not exhaust this   In everything trans-
cendence searches   The dance
step, its stretches, forward
and back, across the thin line
Across its non-existence

civil war   The lashing of Leviathan's tail   Death principle
of nations   Pol Pot's smile; in his jungle monastery
Everything fuses   Principles of codification are compacted; concealed,
the deathtraps of simplification arise   Like ghosts

The shy joy of surprise
in your face, when we arrive
You don't *look* so very ill   You say that
you can see a little patch of sky

We've brought an amaryllis in bloom,
its flowers deep red bells   You have not
yet lost your hair, but I see as if for
the first time that it is gray
You wonder about cancer, where it comes from,
talk about the radon in the alum shale of Ventlinge
I say: We cannot know, there are so many
factors   I see the inner combinatorics   Then
Gustaf arrives, we sit a while longer, then
we leave   The next day was the snowstorm, when I
phone you in the evening you are worse, feel sick
and get a nutrient solution intravenously   You want

to stay in the hospital, are tired, have difficulty
speaking   The cancer-storm blows through your life

XLVIII

We are here with all the dead, their
shadow that always grows   We look in
toward the light that is casting the shadow
Look into the transparent forms of the light

European music is playing
I hear its worlds of sound
cut into one another, as in a counter-
point of worlds   Ricercare   That
conceptual universe   Old
knowledge; old suffering; old phobias
How are we to understand the suffering that exists
when we are not prepared to do anything about it?
The treachery of this   Old treachery
as if it were completely new; risen again

The whirlwind of ash at my feet, invisible
Where shall I set them down?
The firing goes on   We are vessels of clay in the fire

The orders of crime increase in enormity
When did Antigone become genocidal? Creon always was

The rage and the blinding that appear
in large groups of people   The orders of murder
The orders of pain   As if they were logical hierarchies
A Gödel-ladder, where the rungs are knives, razors
or some even thinner blades   Cutting through everything
Through all dimensions   Blood everywhere
In mosques, churches, synagogues, temples, all the thousands of homes
Also in the royal caesura, the whitest center
Not a word, no counter-movement is excluded   Not a single child

And if contemporaneity does not exist   And we are
isolated beings, inside the whirling storm
of confused signs   When we touch one another
we are wholly alien   Then we can breathe   Light   Darkness

The invention of dodecaphony involved
a whole new way of structuring relations
among tones, I said to J   In the architecture
of sound   Which cannot be taken away   Even if
Schoenberg was wrong about the method's
general efficacy   Saw before me the tower of nothing
Then I thought: dodecaphony is also *prayer*, to the one,
                                 the only one, the unimaginable
That which has no image   But it is
only *one* way to pray   There are infinitely many
Trotzdem bete ich   When song comes, in the face of annihilation

there is only one   One single people   My kin
The universal language tells us this   From all directions

XLIX

Now the enclaves are being opened   One after another, where people
have lived shut in, under grenade fire, month
after month, for years   Half-starved, many physically
injured; some with shattered psyches   Children
perhaps forever locked into psychoses
I see their gentle smiles, their helplessness
As if they'd been whirled out into a Hades of Chance
A girl's milk teeth shine   Her eyes be-
speak hopelessness   That which is nameless

The brain's enormously split-up time, in continual
integration, which is itself the prerequisite,
the basis for all integration   Just so, the one is created
Just so, the unity of all life is created   We will suffer the consequences

The human vortices, in the torrent of dreams, uncontrolled
In pain, disappointment, joy   While the ground gives
way; we hang onto trees, other beings
in gliding toward the flux; its ever more powerful surge
The Brownian motion in each human brain;
we construct its order   As if awakened,

fresh, after lovemaking, you say, love   To what?
To what sort of surrender   Time   Silence   Time
The embittered are watching us   As if unable
at any moment to see the lesser evil   I understand them
But I don't want to be like them   Here now is warmth
In the cold that is freedom's I shall love you warm
And you me   Interference   Toward destruction
                              or consummation . . .

L

The sound of C major   We move in toward the stretches
The counter-rhythms   Soon we'll be there; where the great voice
can again go forth   And we are communal unto death
The great caesura opens   Could there be a caesura
of mercy, with the same dimensions as those of
the mass graves? The eyes see us   Things
as they are rise up out of infinity without shadow . . .

The stroke of each caress, to the abyss   Whether dark
or transparent   We shall not know   No stroke is
a caress; not even in its gentlest gesture
Your skin touches mine   Music touches us, with its innermost
                              membranes . . .

LI

How do the strings stretch out toward the stars   Between
them and us are also points of contact, intervals
In these discriminations we exist   Also within their crystal . . .

LII

But among strangers the symbol is broken, in order to be rejoined
Part   Counterpart   We must be everything simultaneously
The world both is and isn't everything that is the case—

We move toward strange planets, strange suns
which are also what is alien within us   This is
the meaning of integration   But we know no integral

Dionysus-Hades dances   I'm speaking with Kore   Her voice
that I always hear
There is no democracy in the underworld   The life of shadows is hierarchical
I speak with the living Kore   Her strength   Her battle

In toward the gray Hölderlin-brain, its enlarged
fluid-filled cavity post mortem   The corpus callosum
very coarse   Bach's Leipzig chorales are playing,
turned inward, in their universal combinatorics
But this is not form   Form exists in every

infinitesimal point, in all senses, in every part of
organization   Where we are constituted, in difference, as individuals

Where justice, too, is born, with the value of its invisibility
All hierarchization pertains to the lowest; also in polyvalence
Even through the walls of nothing in the end we can just see one another
Waves of minorities come in succession
But we need community too, even a community of nothing

Snow fell through the faces of flight; we all want to move
                                        somewhere better
although not even I want to be part of the comparison
Exile is Hades; even from an imagined community
Here one of the criminals sweeps the asphalt path between the houses
                                        as if to demonstrate his worth
Who commits crimes? Those who smash invisible justice
indestructible, transparent, like a wound   From which the tree grows

Against the compulsion to conform   The tree's been there all along
as a barrier   The forms of compulsion even in Social-Democratic
                                        Sweden
That power is gone now   As is the security; in increasing
unemployment   While the systems of social equality
quickly and consciously are destroyed by the bourgeoisie who felt
coerced for half a century   The revanchist energy is
very strong   Those who felt secure had no resistance at first
Now it's coming, in incipient uncertainty   Will it suffice?

This time the degraded and the downtrodden have no

organization

LIII

No one sings all the time   By everything else we shall also be judged

But only we ourselves can do it

This is without exception   We who are everything else   In the dark

song, bright, beyond

all comprehension

Controls come from below, from the given
But that's not where we are   Not now   The crocus opens its petals
to the stars   In what is the burning brain of everything—
That sounds weird   Yes   And it is   Come now
The all burns with its particular fire   We will not put it out

Objective music sounds   Mozart
Ligeti   Or something else, with its remote resonance
The fronts dissolve, the vanquished wait   No mercy
to be found, or not to be found   As if anarchy had no
significance   It's not here that freedom exists
Freedom is action   Not the waiting to be killed, not to be
killed, or something still worse   The triumph of those who commit genocide
Now   In Gorazde   Soon somewhere else   This is completely

repulsive

In the global network come images of the mass murderers,
from the hills they regard their work through binoculars
Cannons shoot directly into the defenseless city, this
time Gorazde, where 65,000 people crowd together
in the center   And their names? Karadzic   Mladic   With their lens caps
off, they see nothing   Least of all themselves
Before which judge shall they stand? How will justice be exacted?
Time's fruit ripens on the tree   Planetary time; green
All the clocks show a slightly different time   Nor are they in
exactly the same place   Searchlights are sweeping   The wave of darkness
runs over the earth   The tidal wave of money; data-gold
From the commuter train tonight I see the moon's lantern, half-full, still waxing
There, beyond the North, the sun is shining; eternally without horizon—

The invisible hand acts at full strength   What were visible hands,
long since parts of it, thus themselves invisible
But music also acts   As if it alone were freedom . . .

As if I could impose the punishment   Within me there is also the sentence
Gray spring   Today I will give someone the help I can give
This will not help me but perhaps it will help her   Thus completeness arrives

LIV

I do not want to be in the comparisons   Where
inner death alone exists   But the fundamentals?

Similarities   Differences   Continuum   Division
The bifurcated storm   Mobile   Immobile
The huge wing will rise up out of the earth
The blue eyelids fall shimmering toward the shores
The white point deepest inside the storm utterly black

The great light unfolds, like rustling silk wings,
from the invisible   Dragonfly wings   Butterfly wings   Or
the wings of the angel of Annihilation   In their transparent darkness
Over and over again the movement for social
justice begins   After all the aborted attempts
The light of genesis   Each time new in its revelation   Epi-
                                        phanies, unavoidable
Return, repetition, not even logically possible . . .

The brutal streak in the young Ezra Pound, when in the face of the war's
                                        mass slaughter
he thought it better if a few at the top were killed . . .   Here
is the entrance to his darkness   The throne of Rhadamanthys shines
dark gold in the darkness   Around it the righteous swarm
                                        But this is of no use

If the language that comes is not language   What
shall I do then? Wait for silence   Language without language
erects its walls   Intolerable heat   Banners of dust

LV

Democracy's secret   In free, general elections, with secret ballots
There, too, is music's concealment, its inaccessibility, eye
to eye   Where coercive power, over the other, does not
exist   This is music's secret   When music moves,
sovereign, in time, its own time   For that is what defines it

South African faces, in the first free election   The dignity,
the joy breaking through, the laughter, the tears   And the wave
of warmth   As if the terrorist bombs, the violence, did not even exist
Amandla! The strength to do what? The power to do what? We shall see—

There's the fear that disappointment will come   Also inside
myself   But that is not I   Objective music sounds
for a moment   That which is history   If that summary word has
                                     any meaning whatsoever
I have been here before   When in the city park in Lund
I took off my hat on the first of May, when we sang
the Internationale, at a Social-Democratic gathering, in the early
'60s   A warm rain fell on my head   New, light-green leaves
That I, too, grasped democracy's secret   The unification of
fellowship and sovereignty   Respect for the worth of every
human being   Later another kind of transparency came, the blinding

Every moment democracy must be won anew   As if
it were always indefensible, defensively   As if it just
existed as light actively moving outward   For a short time it can eliminate

violence   But violence can grow overpowering   As can the violence of others
    against others
This is no excuse   Worth itself is always obliterated by murder

LVI

Objective music   A concept I continually
return to   Or rather: a reality   Because the sound is
inescapable, within me   Because we are
palintropic beings? What are they? Returning, always
recursive, time created again and again, in its interior
spherical form   A hypersphere; of a growing number of dimensions
Memory's recognitions   Near-identity   For we are
never alike   Or: all-too-alike, in our mental automata
But we transcend   The motorics of the fingers moves   The motorics
of the soul   The selfsame movement   Until something breaks out
                                      A wing
From which pair of wings? Birds fly at breakneck speed, in an uproar

New wars   Rwanda   Yemen   San'a' is attacked with Scud-missiles
Bloated corpses float in the turbid river from which
refugees draw water   While spring explodes here
All the flowers, birds   The ash tree's dark violet flowers
In the ravine wood anemones, lesser celandine, and hollow-root, *Corydalis*
cava, rare   Fragrant balsam poplars, grown wild
From the bridge we see a big pike, streaking across
the bottom in shallow water   Full of algae

On the pike's back some kind of thread-shaped growths   Parasites?
A wild duck squeaks   We look for the mourning cloak in the still clear
hazel thicket, but it is not there   The nuthatch calls
In the evening we drink wine, make love, twice
then we watch an old film, 8 1/2, don't watch the news
It doesn't hold up   The circus people can no longer simply move on   *Who*

needs it?

Stravinsky asked, about the new music   The chaffinches are singing
I need the music   I listen to its unfamiliar sounds   There

is no repetition

I hear the resonance of war; its complete brutality; its

abrogation of value

But that's not it   Standing wounded before one another

we can also open . . .

The raging storm takes fire   When the wounds of political
silence open up under the skin   The white
hell opens   All righteousness   All pride   All
shame   At what is on my hands, what
cleaves to me   I am publicly thanked   But I can't
take it   No one has the right to thank me
Yes, it's true, I say, about my having written a poem in 1965
about the war in Vietnam   That I then wrote several more,
took part in the solidarity movement, onward to victory
I add: Those years have left a deep mark on my life   I feel
I'm not being understood; a smile comes to my lips
Earlier I refused to recite the poem   I look at
Bao Ninh, the author of a realistic novel about the war

He sits absolutely quiet, drinks wine   Knows no foreign languages
I myself feel utterly foreign   It is my lot to play host to
all that is foreign   Unconditional hospitality   The conditions are the same
I cannot repeat anything   But I know that I would
do the same thing, again, against that war   I talk about you,
dearest, who had come home in the afternoon and spoken about
a 13-year-old Vietnamese girl you met at a school, who said
there were two things she liked in Sweden: democracy, and
that you were allowed to criticize your teachers   I tell this
to my friends   With official representatives I cannot speak—

For the first time a major reconciliation   Perhaps   Yesterday
Nelson Mandela took an oath as president of South Africa   In a
simultaneous liberation of Africans and Boers   Never   Never   Never
again, shall this beautiful land need to experience oppression, or
suffer the shame of being regarded as the scum of the earth, said Mandela
But we do not know   The white extremists suddenly seem to be few and
marginalized
The strength, the power of transformation   *Amandla*   With the same force as
pain   But in the moment of liberation as if without resistance
The light streaming from people's faces, in lines at
their polling places, with their same human value   *That* strength
But all power is transformed   In the wear, the tear, toward other
attractors   Once before I praised a victory; which became bitter
This time it is something else   Law   Democracy   Peaceful means—
I know, everything simultaneously carries its opposite   As does this reservation

LVII

We flee furiously in the directions of all the senses   Also in nothing's
There is no difference   Even the flame of nothing burns
We are inside the function   There is nothing outside it

As if the wandering between vowels and consonants
were also a wandering between the mountains Parmenides
and Heraclitus, or between the discrete and the continuous

A dance of vowels and consonants; where they also change functions
A generalized pattern of gesture; the movements of the larger body; also
                                                    semantically, conceptually

The play of feelings and of interests   I see the outer
surfaces of faces, the small tic in the cheek,
the darkness passing over the skin, in spite of
all that is said, in languages that lie
Every power struggle is destruction   Breaking apart the
fragile form   Where it issues, free of constraints,
from the captivity that is existence   Dark
matter of the soul; of an indeterminate sort   We are here
only for a short time   On the near-infinite interior surfaces . . .
What is time? That which uses us   In the larger brain—

Vowel lengths are decisive, also of the tension in
interior rhythm   Whichever mountain we leap off; so the
stretto also happens between mountains   Mussels resting

darkly in strata of clay, living, breathing the clear water;
or practically fossils already   Under the increasing weight
Scraping sounds   Explosions of consonants   Vibrating R-notes, grating
The danse macabre of crystals   As if they were already principles   The heart's
freedom breathes—

LVIII

All the irons in the fire   If they are irons   If it is fire—
As a child I saw the irons in the forge   The sputtering sparks
from the anvil . . .
The peculiar comfort of fire   The generalized conflagration
Where will I be when it comes? Will I be defenseless?

The opening for all language, all images, all sound
Only through listening, seeing, speaking-singing can it work
Straight through the stone that shines monstrously   And the terror of the idyll
I touch you with the wing of pain; lightly, lightly, lovingly
Each moral problem carries its inner darkness
The darkness precipitates hatred   It does not have to dominate . . .

Word comes: Yet another of my friends has cancer   I hear his
voice on the telephone, it is not he who tells me about it,
I believe he understands that I know, but we talk about
other things   His intellect is intact, as if the immanence of death
did not touch it at all   We speak about language, about grammar
Analytical or normative   I propose the possibility

that the differently constructed faculties of language in our two cerebral hemispheres
perhaps give rise to two different kinds of syntax, engaging each other
in a dialogue   Within myself I hear the dichotomies, recurrent
on many levels, ontologically, epistemologically   Also
emotionally, perhaps; but I also imagine a kind of tri-
section   A constantly growing number of factors
I remember a sketch I did when I was 18 years old, of a tower constructed
of shards patched together, which was also a plant, or
a rising member   Rising into the invisible counterpart   Then I listen to
the aged voice, hear its liveliness, its acuity, when new thoughts
come to mind   We talk about new poetry; how it is possible to perceive
the exact taste of its language, its edge   That one can go wrong, but this sense is still
                                                                unerring
I realize that soon we will not be speaking with each other any more   This hurts
What have I learned? I have seen incorruptibility, concentration, seriousness
I think about another one of my friends, who died of the same kind of cancer
The same kind of face, when the great music played   The same light, coming from
        inside the face

LIX

How am I to reach the greater integration? It can come only
from what is free of strain; the enormous compactness, its
lightness, its weight . . .   I touch you with the gray wing
I touch your brown cheek with my wing   I saw you
walk among the flowers, among your tall tulips

The glass-clear wave of tenderness; tears that come then . . .
Immortal we are mortal; mortal we are immortal—-

Forms that arise within us   The leap constantly occurs
The translations   The testing out   We risk our lives on
the durability of these forms, their ability to describe
the world   And yet not one of them holds   We see the spent forms, from outside
And yet they were life   No life forms are eternal   This is liberation

Interior theater   What is neither Germany, nor Bosnia   Nor
any other country, not even a utopia   As in a huge
absence; where all seem to sit with their faces turned away
Entre-visages, I thought once, and saw before me
faces turned toward each other, their contacts, through absence
itself, the averted state   We are there alone   With the terror
I hear the wind in the trees in the rain   The sound of all the new leaves
The sound of all the new children   While they are swept into the vortex . . .

The heart bears its simplifications   Its wings rattle
In the burning brain are convection currents of feeling
The burning heart bears its chill, its wrath
Before us new wars, new revolutions   Once
I myself was prepared; in any case emotionally   Intellectual
preparations   The movements of the real were greater by far
I am burned   Gasoline soon extinguishes the burning house

LX

With V I talked about the young heifers in the meadow
As a child she was a shepherdess, tending cows and sheep
She spoke with expertise about the ages of calves   When I said
one of them was a beauty she replied: They are all beautiful!
We spoke about flowers, their names, in Swedish and in Latvian
Our language was English   We spoke about something else, not
politics, not nationalisms, rather about the intense, open
human emotion, love   Virgin Mary's keys are also
Mother-of-God's hand   The whole hand open, fingers spread
We looked at twayblade, and at St. Peter's keys

At Digerhuvudet on Fårö she walked away alone
along the white rubblestone shore, her brown shawl
swept around her head, an old woman, a figure of pain
I also walked away, but in the other direction, in the blinding
light from the stones, the sea, below attacking terns
When I came back to the group I saw her
She showed me her find, a clump of moss the size of a fingertip, gleaming
silver   I showed her mine: a coral shaped like a clam shell, petrified,
                                        four hundred million years old
All we did not talk about   What came after the dictatorship
The conflict of pain   What "the national" is, if other than a fiction
And what in that case this fiction means   I do not know

LXI

Straight through disorientation and death   The near-infinite
landscapes that rise toward the sky and the sea
Flowering meadow saxifrage, a sea of white over the heath
where the curlew takes flight   The lapwing   The oystercatchers
Where burnt orchids, small purple-and-white orchids bloom
And pasque flowers, their little heads   Junipers wander
away into the distance toward infinity   A road   A lighthouse
The series of overtones rises, all the more steeply   Silence
We have inner thresholds of velocity, thresholds of comprehension
Time's limits, upward and downward; limits of integration
Humans; we move in real landscapes
beyond all models   Including those we make of our-
selves   Infinite fineness does not suffice—

We will approach maturity   So many of my friends are dying now
Are dying or already dead   I listen to the pain, the
fragile limit of the voice, clear   Then come the hiccoughs, the lump
in the throat, the small touch of valor   I try
to just be there   Consolation is impossible   What could I
possibly have to offer   I hear my own voice vibrate

Into the white storm-space   Nothing has
changed there   Out there is only storm, invisibly
racing clouds, surging trees of pain, on every leaf a
face, mutable, as if on a small gold screen
Mirrors of metal, burnished   Water   Clear as glass   Within the whiteness a

distant black point, rapidly approaching   Out there
across the sea   I hear its roar   The scent of salt   Seaweed
I too flee for protection   But it doesn't help

Rwanda   The picture that comes into focus more and more clearly   One of
the larger genocides, also of this century
Churches have been transformed from asylums into abattoirs   Everywhere
corpses lie, rotting bodies   Children   Women   Men
The numbers are always growing   The radio station of the Hutu extremists
broadcasts nonstop exhortations "to exterminate the cockroaches,"
the Tutsis   An officer in the Tutsi guerrillas speaks of Auschwitz,
that Europeans also gave themselves to such pursuits
It is still going on   The smaller genocide in Bosnia goes on
The suffering is immeasurable   We count the dead
Maybe we should count the living   Our guilt grows and grows
Not collective guilt; but personal responsibility

LXII

The roads full of traffic   All the vehicles, on their way somewhere
All the messages   A dense crowding of frequencies
Ships on their way   All the freight   All the people
I see their shining oboli; concealed, or revealed

Little bird-Anna, in the hospital bed   In a thin, white
angora sweater, right on her skin   And with blue
cotton trousers   Almost no hair on her head, gray

The hot-and-cold body, sweaty, when we embraced
The conversation goes partly astray, as if you'd
lost the thread, but in between you're entirely
lucid   Your eyes have changed, the whites are a different color,
and their expression, almost as if coagulated
But your smile is the same, shy, timid, complete
You are in your death throes   You dance your last, sovereign dance

I will speak with you a long time, Anna, even
when you are dead   I hear your voice
very clearly, how you phone me,
and say: It's Anna   Yesterday I saw your soul
on the day of your death, moving in toward a great light,
that was there beyond the trees, where I was walking in the woods
The sun also shone, in the evening, on the grasses and the bluebells
The white bedstraw was fragrant   A mouse scampered across the road, darkly
The great function is in your voice, as if embedded
in the function of all functions   They cannot be formalized
They radiate beyond all time   They bear the light of time
That's how we are embedded   Today I saw the blue vault of the heavens
In all directions is blue space, in its darkness
That is where we come from   That is also where the light comes from
We also carry one another's light   I want to carry it a short way
How long I can do it I don't know   The weight, the lightness is enormous
You know this too   Your voice vibrates, hovers   The sound opened to-
ward God's world   Everything could be heard differently   I will
be there, in the new interpretations   Earth, expanded, is greater

LXIII

Down toward the stream, its flow, I play a wooden flute
I play sorrow   The tones are difficult to balance, heavy pressure
is needed; I bend the notes, touch other scales   In the tone
is also a rasping sound   This bird moves quickly

Anna Rydstedt now rests in her grave at the foot of the Alvar,
south of the church tower in Ventlinge, her head toward
Kalmarsund   There she rests on her journey   I was a pallbearer, I carried
the coffin out of the church through the side door, out into blinding sunlight
I was thinking: Now we're carrying you out feet first
When we lowered the coffin into the grave the swifts came, shrilling, in wide arcs
The coffin came to lie a bit lopsided, so you lean slightly against your left side
But I imagine this sets your head erect, on your journey out into the light
And so we say farewell, all of us   Many have come a long way, then we travel
                                        in different directions
On your coffin lay a limestone chip with a yellow lichen, xanthoria, a small
shard of black shale, the shell of a garden snail, birdfeathers   There was
also an arrangement of wildflowers and, I believe, grasses
The colors blue and yellow and yellow-brown   Nearest the limestone
                                        earth was laid
I think about the earth's journey   We are all parts of it   The red ship
in the fresco inside the church travels from west to east   Your journey
is now toward the west   We are all in the land of sunset and sunrise

LXIV

another bird, that flew upward, in the Forum Romanum
up toward the Rostra   Maybe a serin, but
I don't know   Flowers were in bloom, flowers I don't recognize
What may have been acanthus, growing like lupins
And a red flower, close to the ground   White butterflies
At the house of the Vestals roses bloomed   Up above
the palace and the ruins of villas a falcon flew
Sudden silence of birds   At what sort of rostrum do what sorts
of speakers appear   I listen to the voices of Europe
I feel no confidence; not even in my own distrust
STEER! We all carry the sparkling diamond oar
Hard; like the gates of Hades   Shadows full of unrest
The Curia, restored in the '30s, in the face of new imperial power
Which senate meets there; which tribunes of the people, if they would now
have audience, even in Hades   We move through the centuries
Faced with destitution's images   The blood of the martyrs is clasped, cradled
As if Agave were clutching the head of Pentheus; the blood runs
down into a bowl; a grail   The Etruscan votive sculptures
are thin as sticks; are by Giacometti   What do the dead
see? What do they see that even the dying do not see? What
Hesperian fruits, shining   Pomegranates; golden fruits?
By the Baths of Diocletian are orange trees   Hidden
inside there, Michelangelo's basilica, is full
of power, stone-dead, of the living   Small flames burn for believers
Policemen stand in groups, some with bulletproof vests, submachine guns
The door to a bordello stands open   Private health clubs

with sauna, massage   At Stazione Termini are all kinds of people;
from all over the planet   Everything stands wide open, glowing poverty
A beggar woman, emaciated, a shawl over her head, a half-
grown child in her arms, also sleeping, does not wake when you give
her money   Which ones listen   Which hear the invisible voice   The one
with no platform, no altar, who is not even heard at the sacrificial spring in the under-
world, welling up from the rock; clear green water   You want
to touch the water, but I stop you   Maybe it is also
polluted? We go to the Colosseum, sit there together
on a marble bench, the fragment of one, behold the endless stream
of tourists   Shadows in the planetary Hades; we among them
On the Palatine there's a wedding; we talk to the cats a while   Look at
more flowers, butterflies   One wholly ordinary sparrow, but a little different
In our hotel room afterwards we make love; fiercely, with great intensity

LXV

As if nothing but the real-infinite *were*
That beyond our comprehension was
the white ocean storm, I read, formulated somewhat
differently, in a passage of Kant   About this
I have always known   Also about the dark
point in the storm   About the great and the small
I have been at the extremes, not just in a dream   The one
that burst what little reality I owned
That was a long time ago   What do I have now?
The social surrounds us, like an alien

reality; the resultant of a large number of vectors
is always alien; a trivial fact, so difficult
to understand   This looking inward also becomes limited
But nothing is unaltered   We are expert at change
As if we always had the brain of a child, even unto death

I hear the childish music   I hear my own voice's
song; its vocalics, its rasping, explosions

In this counterpoint   What do I make of the social
I touch the lives of those closest to me   Song touches
everyone, even in foreign languages   We are differentiated
We shall not be integrals, not even in the alien eye of God
Society moves chaotically, toward simpler and simpler controls
where local variations cancel one another out   It is
unstable; that is where our freedom lies; that which is beyond
all controls   Like the oceanic storm, white   Or black   Everything
changes place with every other thing   I feel your soft lips, smell your
scent, in an unparalleled familiarity   You are not alien, or
in any case least strange of all   We argue with each other
We make love with each other, softly   We love each other   The curtain
billows through the window, a stronger gust of wind opens a slit between them
The leaves strike one another, the panicles of the grasses move   A flower fly
stands still in the air   A distant bird is audible again   Which
bird? Impossible to hear! It is part of life alien to us
At twilight the song thrush sang   Softly, softly   In fragments of
the rhythms of Mozart, what resembles them   Now several birds   A warbler?

The small gray bird down by the bridge? Among the shimmering blue dragonflies . . .
Yesterday I played the flute for the dead woman   Down toward the streaming

water—

LXVI

We are in the perpetually damaged language   And will
remain there, so as not to become monsters   That's where
the given is broken, and new form becomes possible
I hear new birds   The song thrush sings
at the break of day   Weak, weak light,
the song perfectly clear   Now it's day, other birds
From the neighbor's house up in the woods we hear hammer blows
A car passes on the road   On television we see
the political elites, their awkward dance   There are
also other elites, more invisible   I do not want to
belong to any of them   Because they are defined
Also self-defined; in their regnant power
Which is the opposite of the form of the elective, in love
There is almost nothing without form   Form chooses us
In the evening I gaze into the abyss of genetic technology
How the groundwork for the human is literally pulled out from under us
There, too, art is deep as an abyss   For we have no
choice   The logic of this research can no longer be halted   Only
deflected or diverted like an unusable
flue in a chimney   We will find ourselves amidst monstrous births

Those who believe they can select life away
don't know what they're talking about   The form of the abyss is so much
deeper   The pain goes so much deeper   *Hoi polloi kakoi*, defined
away as shit, in their immense numbers   So many, that
not even the mapping of the human genome
will go very far   In this immense combinatorics   In this
comparatively simple form's living, growing response to the world
in its experienced, its lived totality   Which is not totality
For that cannot exist   Whosoever does violence to the unfinished
does violence to infinity   One cannot do this without dying
This is what death is, outer or inner   I look at
the minute latticework in the wings of the blue damselfly   That which
breaks the light   The shimmering richness   We find ourselves amidst radiant change
We are not shit   We are the many   We bear luminous wounds
We bear the possibility of love; also its real sweetness   Its sound

LXVII

Always alone   For otherwise the life of the fragile
symbols dissolves   In what we do together
giving occurs; and symbols of a different kind
are born   In this there is war   As if conditions of peace
were contaminated at every moment   A delicate balance
Deep peace   At night I dream of snakes;
vipers, of different colors   Your face
looks at me   I am anti-social; cannot participate   This is my
stigma; inscribed as a snakebite   I bear the crescent moon

I also bear you, beloved   As my living sign
How do I become a sign for you   I reproach you for your goodness
Thus I am evil   From the cave my dream is also born:

                                        a single god, colorless,

                                                    with no face
Then the light from within is lit   We illuminate the world   Crystal!

LXVIII

Mozart's music comes as forms of liberation
through our inner ocean darkness   Everything has suddenly
eased, before new cramps arise, new waves
of parrying rage, with its shriveling light that is all too
clear, which is but a form of darkening
How is love possible through this warding off?
It doesn't work   Perhaps we should be in the music of vulnerability
Mozart also touched on the esoteric tradition,
but extracted from it only humanity   He *was* chosen,
did not need to delimit himself, never was instrumental,
never held people in contempt, except those who entered other people's lives
with violence   Resistance is not delimitation
All human experience is relevant   For we can never
know in advance what is pertinent   Sometimes not even afterwards
What was it that happened to us   The dark tower   The tower of
zero, stands there still, its pillar black   There I stand,
a counter-alchemist, even, as it were, with my hands charred black

Chemistry exists only in a small interval   The full spectrum is so much larger
The immensely many exist in their oceanic movement, in their birth—

LXIX

At night once more the moon's quiet, mystical light
The moon is in the trees in the forest, no wind at all   No one sees it
but me, from inside the sleeping house
Now a light breeze moves stiff leaves in the heat
What does human light have to do with me? Have I
turned away, esoteric; though this was never my choice
I don't know   I cannot abjure inner sovereignty
Which is also external   I taste blood
in my mouth, on my lips   Who am I sacrificing?
For whom shall I become an offering? Perhaps no one   Not even for that
would I be of any use   But I shall touch you with life . . .

LXX

Now the dead call to me from out at sea, where the sun sets
over the tongue of land, in violet haze   Around the sun two rainbow fragments,
like widely spaced quotation marks   It's as if the dead could now also
meet   While we, the survivors, walk on the shore
Everything is only provisional   The sea moves calmly   Terns fly
along the water line, its irregular form   New
sandy beaches are forming; at intervals briefer than I could have imagined

Other stones lie there, more than a thousand years
We are in the presence of the order of permanent murder, its smaller
eternity; and thus not eternal   Its abolition is on the agenda
For us and for those who survive us   For all the dead!
New bladder wrack moves in the clear water   Women are swimming, a few
of them   In the distance the city is visible, where I first saw the order
Freedom's wing also came from there   Like a measurement from inside   From the
opened order . . .

LXXI

The stiff leaves scrape against one another like metal
in the breeze, in the rising heat
A distant bird   A flower fly buzzes
How does a cosmic blossoming become possible?
How will life here be passed on
in the mother row of hypercycles, in a growing
cosmic summer   At night I see the star above the top of the spruce
In the forest moisture rises   The little waterfall in the stream,
its rushing, now only like a gently purling spring
as in the Mithraic temple under San Clemente in Rome
How can we touch the wellsprings of the galaxies?
During the day I look at the dragonflies over the meadow, something
more than ephemeral creatures, *Aeschna grandis*, with its
wings shimmering copper, its brown-and-light-blue abdomen
The regal gold-ringed dragonfly, yellow and black   The gold skimmer, sparkling green
The Libellulidae, the blue broad-winged damselflies, a red damselfly

Also a large blue dragonfly, I wonder if it isn't
the emperor; it could also be something else   Butterflies
are few this year   Grasshoppers rasp   You see a brown viper
vanish beneath the foundation of the house, where you water the roses
after having freed them of nettles   Crayfish get into the eel-trap
How do we take care of the living? My mother says she heard
on the radio that there hasn't been a summer as warm as this in 80 years
The summer of 1914, I think, with forest fires, cosmic signs
My mother was a little over a year then; later she got the Spanish
flu, which she barely survived; until the turn in her breathing came
and death's threshold retreated   The sun rises burning
It's hard to take care of the living   The dead only apparently easier
What is lacking in my love? Isolated gray hawkweeds remain, shining
                                                    yellow-white

LXXII

to the burning brain   Everything is already burned down
Shimmering   The antennae of the brimstone butterfly have a pale violet tinge
I see, when it alights on a climbing rose, the same color as the
small spot at the center of the wing . . .

Again literally at nothing, although I know
it cannot exist   And yet nothing *is*, in its monstrousness
In the black currant bush I find a moth, with small tufts of hair on
its thorax, like small ears, barbs   On the brown and gray wings
a sign, intensely yellow   I look it up: *Autographa gamma*

What kind of darkness do I see before me
It is not merely social   The destruction of
human bodies and souls will
continue; in their luminous beauty   This is
humanity's predicament   It is another darkness
That which is not yet well-known, defined
I feel its attraction   See the signs
that point toward it, as toward a higher consciousness
Which it isn't   Maybe it also has a human form
I look up toward the stars through binoculars in the still luminous night
The dark trees move slowly   In the morning, their surge, growing
in the gray heat, before the front comes with its thunder and rain
with the shifting light that bodes darkness . . .
Then I play Haydn's music, hear its clarity,
as if it were completely utopian, and it is
Reconnecting to the 18th-century dream, enlightened, liberal . . .
The immanence of enormity   Also Swedenborg's dream of green, o-
                                        pened buds
We are in the darkness of Mozart, its obsession with death, while the starlings cry
As if we again should be led to the Cave, with the shadows of light
Even the unique, the sovereign individuals, with their inviolable value,
bear their own darkness, infinitesimally . . .   What is it we are singing?

LXXIII

A human world I could relate to vanishes
with unheard-of speed   Help me, so that
I too don't vanish   The abstract universe
once came to me in a dream, as the utmost
concretion   Help me, so that I can be loving

The unending, glass-clear surface inside me was also the
desert outside   Only when I touch someone else is there a boundary
What will I do when the others die? How will I go on?

Get ready for the challenge   Remove everything that's in
the way   Practically   Also physically   Then I'll have to
see   For there is nothing I can predict   The future
literally does not exist, least of all as a letter
Slowly the sign grows, more and more complex, more and more clear

The song has the right to be wrong   But this grants no right
to absolution   We stand before the imageless
In the dream I bend over a spring, kidney-
shaped, or shaped like a heart   Its mirror is shimmering,
metallic lilac   Every image is annihilated there
I shall descend there, go through it   For this image is not
the imageless   Nor are the forms of the invisible without image
Presence is invisible   Nor do I know if this is a projection
What I shall find in the underworld of the invisible I cannot know
Whatever I mean by this underworld   The realm does not exist   What am I singing?

Forgive us all our dead   Forgive us all our living
Forgive all the living   For the dead there is no forgiveness
Who is it that will forgive? Who is it that will be forgiven?
Can I forgive your forgiving me? Do you forgive yourself?
No! We cannot apportion grace   For the living there is no forgiveness

LXXIV

In what way do psychic realities remain?
Parts of all that vanishes   Farther and farther away
As if all time could be stored in one single memory,
one single brain! This exists in feeling
but probably nowhere else   All time exists in the future
I once imagined, without really knowing
what I meant   We enter the realm of the irremediable,
as if entering a Hades that is continually being born

The big ash trees shine in front of the dead woman's house, soon
no longer hers   The sheep are in the *horva*   Along the shore
of light she rides bareback, her long hair flutters, the horse's
mane flutters   Black shale protrudes from the fault scarp

In the core words of light, night suddenly opened
Even the word "light" and the word "night" appeared to be
compromised   No single word excepted   But I
knew that! Still, turmoil comes, disorientation
The gray earth opens   The gray wing appears

The journey proceeds through a late-summer landscape under the architecture
    of clouds,
up through Roslagen, beyond the big paper mill
The old man makes his way downstairs, his body emaciated,
his eyes full of life   We talk about the soul   The Hebrew soul,
ruach, the Greek soul, *psyche*, about Freud's *Seele*; in Freud
the subconscious is in the soul   That in Judaism and in early Christianity
there is no life after this one, that resurrection should occur in the flesh,
or in cosmic restoration   A neighbor comes in with a big salmon,
from the sea outside; a big female with masses of roe; Ingegärd tries
to slice the salmon but doesn't quite manage   Then she grabs hold
of its head, I cut, hit the knife with a hammer; Karl sets
the slices aside, I'm afraid of cutting his fingers   He no longer feels sick
to his stomach, he says, now he eats ordinary food, but what nauseated him earlier
thoroughly disgusts him now, raspberries and blueberries for example   We eat a
cake made from pulped zucchini   I ask if he is in pain   Yes, sometimes, he
says, moving his hand toward his side, but I'm taking painkillers   Then I
drive home, before he grows too tired   The three of us stand outside the house,
look at the kitchen garden, the big birch tree, a lightning notch in its trunk
I'm in traffic that gets increasingly dense   Birds of prey float over the edge of the woods
I feel the contingency of this land   The language   How we live our lives

Bengt A's voice, it uttered not a word, but I heard in its intonation
exactly what it wanted to say   About honesty   About not
compromising   About remaining in one's astonishment   I wanted to have told him
about the hawfinch chick, shaggy, with a massive head, thick bill   How I
watched it try to crack open a cherry stone, and I realized

it was no ordinary chaffinch   Only through feeling does exactness
come, I understand later   I myself must be the instrument
Thus only modern instruments exist, even if they're ancient
Digging them up out of graves is not possible   The dead shall be dead
Only thus do they become alive   No new music rises up out of graves

LXXV

And if the song becomes atrocious? It has the right to be
No part of what is human can be censored
I gaze into petrifaction's eyes   Is this also
a part of me? Am I a part of atrocity?
Yes! Without a doubt! There's no wax I can plug
my ears with   The ropes of the winds bind me, even if
with a wind of mirrors   Continual   Whirling shards

We set out on the dark sea; under a blinding sun; under
the sun of death   No house can be restored
Nor any brain   We move into the space of the unknown; none
other   Are universal and particular   We can't exclude
any one of the mountains of being   Sun   Sea   Rock   A society,
always growing, even as it goes under   How can we go on loving?
There are no descriptions   Nor any of their correlatives
All that exists is this living reality, born out of the two   As if
this were our reality, in all its blindness   Simultaneously sweet . . .

Beauty   Repulsion   I must not deny any feelings
I have a right to my disbelief   I pledge allegiance to the contaminated
world, such as it is, in its luminous right . . .

What sort of imaginary community do I seek? Which one
is active, est agens, within me? I project the collective Sade!
The collective Mozart! As if there were no difference!
Summed up in the Gödel-face, dark   Beneath the real Gödel's
shy gray shadow   In which group do I seek protection? Whom am I
excluding? Which flame of self-forgiveness consumes me?
Societies float gently, like ashes   An architecture of smoke

LXXVI

The luminous, pulsating web   Strange   The light that comes
from within, an impenetrable substance   The wall is the
impossible; what we must pass through, not
all the possibilities   Skin? Cerebral matter? Other tissue? As if this
were the substance of God; whatever I mean by that   Illumination from within
is real   Even were it part of the imaginary universe   Infinite

LXXVII

Not in vain do you give me your rose   The transparent forms
are reborn; from them everything arises   All leaves, birds
All the images   Growing quickly, quickly destroyed

I will not let you down   A flower opened your heart
Now you open mine, again, with your rose, shining dark red
The yellow pollen from eternity's sunflower falls on the table

LXXVIII

When the vision came, the vision of the all, the vision of infinity
there were no images, not even a sea, not even the
geometry of the impossible   Only this horror that *is*
The images that came were approximations, making this endurable
That is why images are consumed   That is why they are melted down
That is why the images of this language also are consumed, even its very least sign
Even its differentiated silence

Down there, at the bottom, at the center of the abstract . . .
That's where tentative movements, shoots, membranes exist
between different abstract spaces, their molecular substrates
Different kinds of beings, different kinds of life, rest side by side

You who came into my center   You gave me
your breast to kiss, though you never before allowed anyone

to kiss your breasts   Tenderness opened for me
Its enormity   I've been inside there ever since, in what
became open earth   The infinitely opened brain

Before the judgment   Whether temporary or final
I don't know   Stillness inside me   If only I could be *Kerylos*,
and we could fly together, halcyonically, across
the darkest water, entirely still, in the center of the storm . . .

LXXIX

Now I take a public stand, in the battle over the European house,
in the battle over the European brain   I say no to
this country's, Sweden's, entering into a political union
based on the Maastricht Treaty   Because for me this
means giving up one kind of political democracy—
such as has existed in this country—to obtain another   A kind
of influence, gained by lobbying the great powers, through
the agency of the hollowed-out state   It is not a no to
Europe, I think and also say, wondering what I mean

We are universal, or nothing at all   Europe, too, has
the right to exist   I see the rifts, the abysses, crys-
tal-clear   A blue-white light   Murder exists,
but has no right to   What is right is something else;
we gather ashes, here everything is irradiated with pain—
From one of the new ghettos comes music, piercing

It's unintelligent to see the opponent as unintelligent
It is also inhuman   No external power affects what takes place
in a brain   Everything that comes from outside is transformed
Internal violence exists   That's what comprises the fire—

LXXX

Dance is born out of the deepest interior of our bodies   As if the light there
were streaming out, out of each body part's smallest movement
We hear gasping breaths   We behold mouths open in trance
Out of them light also issues, in the whirling darkness

The stone falls through millennia   The clear water's darkness
deeper and deeper   But the vanishing is only apparent   The
construction of enormity grows and grows   In its transparency

Pain's nadir, deeper and deeper   At its zenith
Identification with pain, annihilation of pain, is impossible
And yet it's there   Like the entrance into darkness
May I touch *your* darkness? I would so like to

Forms of power move in the invisible   Even
the anti-empire has power, I understand   Together
we have the power to sublate power, I im-
agined once   Even if only within ourselves

But there is no way to place oneself outside   Night has no limit
It is toward infinity I want to go   Unimaginably

What takes place in this thinking substance? The play of the mind's
faculties, the dance, across the inner, shimmering surfaces
For me there was no limit   For me there is no
limit, except at the instant of snapping, even were it
endlessly stretched   We will meet in the silence, after the dance

What does the voice communicate? As if I never knew
in advance   It comes with all its potentials
Invisible   Out of its fold, foldings, a face peers
as if it were Harlequin-Mozart   The great darkness of the eyes! Also
their smile   Quick, friendly   We can be like that too
My vision is now given to the Eye-Brain   Yours, you who
look at me, out of your femininity, half turned away, almost with
your back to me   So that we will not burn up? I hear
your voice   It exists in the vast play of the voices, their light

What kind of movement up from death? Is such a thing possible at all?
A flame rises from the ashes, dances, offers itself, its body
in its moments of stillness, a prayer   Coiling into itself
Unwinding again   Returning to the ruins of silence

LXXXI

Consumed by catastrophe? No! But taking in everything
simultaneously doesn't work   Just do it!
Thus even the crystal cave splits open, in an impossible
birth   No one can divine the new music
Potentialities rest, shining darkly, like embryos
Because something can be treated as finished doesn't mean it is

Rolling Artaud heads, dark, in the unknown
I move within the crystal cranium   Seek in despair
a liberation, an interval of rest   Until I see where I am:
on this foreign stage, the world   We look at one another
a little from the outside, even when we mimic one another

Identification takes place in the frontal lobes   We integrate
death as well   Massacre follows upon massacre,
these too in a mimesis   We mutilate one another's bodies
I don't want to! Nor will I participate in murder
But we are in this whether we like it or not
Images of flowers come to me, fragile birds' eggs
speckled in their nest, near the water   There is no structure more
durable   Time is structure   The dark time   The time of blinding

LXXXII

How to reach into your innermost fragility? Screens drop down very
quickly   Inside there is a glimpse of a swallow's wing
I follow the eye of pain, straight into pain's crystal

I shall approach the colorlessness of nothing, its color
I shall do so with joy, as if approaching
your face   I saw you move, saw the grace of your body
You're illuminated from within   The movements of your limbs
You're about to explain something that deeply moves you, that makes
                                             use of your love
I look at you from the far side of everything   Even from there
                                             I can walk

What is it that shall break through the first integration?

The face has no end   We move toward the face of infinity
The face bears its deep transparency, its pulsating resistance,
until we both come, arriving in a single cry . . .

LXXXIII

As in catatonia   Alien stars are looking at me
It is I who am alien   This is how it will be

Where is my own voice? Where is my own lie? For we don't
live in the truth   I hear a story about someone
who didn't dare speak, for fear of losing her job   It's only
human, I hear myself say to her   At the same time I see
her face, her body, burning, invisibly, on the bonfire
Around us, around the burning stake, are strings of
eyes, in their multitudes, straight through the conflagration
How shall we touch the blood of the stars without fear   Even if
they are inner stars   Between us are invisible bonds

Gliding layers of water beneath an unstable Europe
I have been there before   What magical dance will help?
None   We shall dance, though, with the lives of our bodies
We'll approach the limit   Cross over into darkness

                                        New hatred: crowds of people
screaming on screens, across streets   In which third world?
                                    In which first?

I speak with a close friend   He imagines Europe,
the European Union, as a real peace project,
as a real project for freedom and democracy—
And if it is? What then is the meaning of my no?
The divergence of our visions strikes terror   What am I fighting?

The battle I wage is from within another empire   But I shall be in
the interregnum   Between reigns   I'll fight against reasons for fear

Images that blind? Mirages? How could I possibly know in advance
Perhaps not afterward either   I am one who is never secure

LXXXIV

Mozart of Pain   Madness's Mozart   Mozart sticking out his tongue
My dance   Straight through all the brain's walls   In that which is
generalized connection   Epileptically   Calmed

I'm thinking about her, who listened to music
to soothe the twitching in her face
Now I see that face   Wholly calm

LXXXV

Into which conversations do I enter? Into which psychotic necessity?
History's movements are extremely delicate   And can be
as rapid as within a brain   Everything was transformed so quickly . . .

As if the ground were pulled out from under my existence to this point in time
The folding structures just fall   We do not feel
the land beneath us   Something else begins, over there
The empire? Some other sort of city? Babylon?

It exists in time's rising function
That which has unknown numbers   As if values

were interchangeable   But they are not   The
glass-clear form rises, up from the trench of time
As if it were a continual resurrection,
but with discrete values, exact, complete

Utopias and dystopias gather   Rest like shards
around the radiant forehead   The birth of a head?
We watch this with the eyes of monsters, filled with fear
What are we afraid of? Dying to a further extreme?
No! But I do not want to kill   The empire of nothing
rises with identical counts of the living and the dead   Rapidly
Slowly   But the eyes of the tortured and the humiliated?
Yes   They look at us   I wait for all that builds up inside me,
also innermost in the city of crystal   Where I am not

In which city do I want to be? I want to be in the face
between the realms   I want to touch your hot face
Passing infinitely between realms, I touch your nightgown,
the one you left on the banister while I was sleeping
We are in the house of the real   It is raised up from below

LXXXVI

Since I cast my vote all certainty vanishes, all my interior charge,
as through a trapdoor   I say to myself:
It's right to open oneself up to distrust, to doubt
In this way I shall be inside myself   For

and against   Con-sonant   However much it hurts
Music demands this   If it's to retain any kind of
credibility   Even this I'll distrust
The enormous trees continually give pain its form

Inside me, as if the Mozart-brain
stood wide open, in the third stage of time
Is there a fourth, a fifth?
Something inside me extends across the trembling water
What's flying in there, as if on vanishing wings?
Maybe just death   I talked to my father
I say that I don't know   I stand by that lack of knowledge,
as if it were the only thing alive . . .

The sleep of reason produces monsters   We are bound by
the logic of polarization   Old friends, we look into one another's
transparency, when we are forced to answer, yes or no
In the end I can't say anything, but that it
just disgusts me   When something is forced upon me
I say no   Only afterward can something else become possible
I look into the eyes of the monster   The eyes are full of fear

LXXXVII

Your wing, that carries me
My wing, that would carry you

LXXXVIII

The white, scintillating light   From roofs of frost,
from naked branches, from the thin white coating
on the bark, over purplish brown birch twigs, not yet attuned
to the light of spring   It's still November   I enter in-
to new transformations   In politics   In the economy

I shall try to enter into listening, here as well   To res-
onate while listening   Even to the point of shattering
Which can also be in delight   Even your voice is audible

What's human cannot be preserved   Nothing of me can exist
As if all meanings existed within the huge brain, in a sea-birth
All time comes into being   What returns is never time, only its
                                    shadows, in its blinding . . .

The night countenance sparkling with pain   Sparkling with all of its stars
As if each star were one possible fate
We exhausted the cosmic pictures long ago
We may yet have nothing but this star-birth
These lost children   This trembling love's heart

Eyes that touch one another with their gaze   We literally
look into one another's brains   Into
analogy, sublime, the radiant iris of truth . . .
Seeing also the gray, transparent framework, the construction
of what *is*, in Being   As if nothing did not exist

Or in Becoming   Then I see the forms of time, Time . . .
As if the functions of description ceaselessly changed places
around this vision, in coordinate systems perpetually interchanged,
shifting algorithms, shifting representations, unfinished,
around the invisible center   Your heat looks at me . . .

LXXXIX

Into the haptic cloud   Into its crystallization of time, fluid
The light of the icons touches me, glows   All of its colors   All of its trees
Plastically the light touches me   As if from polyhedrons of higher dimensions
Perfect form does not exist   The rise all the more precipitous
This exhilaration even unto death   Which does not mean war . . .
We want peace   We look at those who kill one another   Why don't we stop them?
This deep divide   As if the continent of being were a caesura
                                        between abysses of time—

In the paper I read an article about power, about the absence of power
giving rise to the violence of anarchy, to the warlords', to the Mafia's
use of violence, at the local level, centering on limited group affiliations
I read that well-defined borders are now lacking in Europe   I think about
        the European
Security Conference, whose voices I heard, in what was then considered
a permanent Europe; back then I distrusted them   Thinking they did not know what
power was   My distrust was justified   Neither did I foresee the dissolution
of one social formation of the order of permanent murder   But European borders

also dissolved, without security, with violence, in what was once Yugoslavia
Germany furthered this process, like a sleepwalker, in an eternal return
This is where we are now   Violent battles in Bihac   Sarajevo up against its third
winter of siege   The violence of national groups undiminished in strength
Genocide continues, if only on a low flame   Serbian nationalism   Croatian nation-
alism
Bosnian sprouting forth   But we must be cosmopolites   In the deep Cosmos
there is no order   In what is most deeply randomized information is infinite
We are hewn out of this infinity   Series upon series   We are in the order of the rose,
in its human vortex . . .

XC

Even the empire crushed from within gathers its shards again
Chechnya   Burned-out tanks on the streets of the capital
still smoldering, soldiers in motion   People, on their way in the rain
From the empire's invisible center new signals go out
Making themselves heard in Bosnia as well   On the surface bordering on
the other empire   Also in
its fragmented organization . . .
Even this country, Sweden, is now a part of the empire
Now we also become a part of the empire's collective power
I myself want to be outside the boundary
Freedom's extremity is tested by what is not yet defined

I lived in the underworld of catastrophes   Beside the concrete garage in Hades
We have only the human lives we have   They are all compounded

I will fight for every shard of democracy
As if no resignation existed, no emptiness
You asked: how was it there, was it very run down   No,
I answered, it was rather tidy, a neighborhood typical
of social group 3   Then it struck me that the concept of the social group
has almost entirely disappeared from the language, following the concept of class
That this has now disappeared in silence   The actual grows in silence
This class struggle still exists   In the battle between invisible classes

The intensity of murder changes   We see the shadows
Hear the cries   As if the intensity of tremendousness also grew
in darkness   Naked existence   Although it cannot exist . . .

Parts of the world's violence? Yes, there's no escaping this
Neither abdicating nor usurping power helps
Weapons are everywhere   Angels fly everywhere
We cut into one another's transparent bodies
Automatic weapons automatically release   The blood is transparent
How shall I seek transnational form   Who are my allies?

XCI

The sum of all blindings   How do I gain entry? How do I
we get through? As if there were but one blinding-brain   How do I touch
its leaves, its butterfly forms   It is night   Only then is light visible
For whom do the blinding stars appear? The stars of darkness—

In darkness it will come   In the lucent darkness
How can I know? I cannot know   That's what darkness is
Only there are we alive   Only there does new light become alive
as if it came from voice, from living voice, water . . .

But the burning brain is in all human beings   It sets the house ablaze
Those still alive are already shadows   Enclosed in fire

XCII

A society rushing away from equality   And which has chosen
this path; also away from democracy   Already subjected
to the democratic deficit of its central structures,
to the Secret Committees of the elites, locally, centrally . . .

How to emerge from my obsessions? The caesura
of sex opens in my brain   That's where I want to be, kissing its
lips   Smelling its fragrance, tasting it   The faint, bitter taste
amidst its sweetness   I seek your sleep that I may awaken

What am I to do with the sexual empire? It has its
power; we are in its force field   But we are not vassals
ANAX   ANASSA   If not, then never mind   *Kitharodoi*; if only with
the instruments of our bodies; the souls of our bodies
For we are in this game, this game of chance   Beyond death

My voice is no longer equal   This is the meaning of vassalage
Do I accept this   No   Every day value is re-created   Until it
is no longer possible   We are in this order   Order there is none

XCIII

Which is the symbolic form that's approaching   In an impossible
topology   All faces touch one another   With their
light, or their darkness   This is what we must understand

Farthest down in darkness I touch the skin of light, touch its
splintering stars   All the signs look at us   Their sound
The time of stars is part of the time of our bodies   Enters into new form
We are in the air of the indefinite   That's where new laws are born
We shall violate them as well   Until we ourselves are destroyed

And if we cannot be renormalized   If we actually are
in real infinity   Where literally nothing
can be strange, not even the music of nothing . . .
And so I take a deep breath, breathe in all that is strange . . .
Where we'll meet one another without fear, in that house

Even at light's lowest level there's splendor, the invisible rose-form
of the brain, in its flowing geometry, whirling   We are
literally measurements of earth   In its unheard-of
pulverization   Invisible dust   New forms of time,

giving birth, in those successively born, in the mother row—
Today, on this day, at this hour Kerylos and Alkyon fly . . .
The white, invisible storm, also has an eye

The delicate branches of the trees move in the gray wind   The brain's
tree moves   Or takes some other form   We are informed
by the real; what can break through the transfigurations of the lie
Technologies of the lie keep being developed   Virtual history,
what has never existed, becomes in the next moment real
The lie steps in and shapes the real   In an indissoluble
confusion, lethal   The mountains, the maxima, in this always growing
                                                complexity . . .
How do we cross over, with which wings   The wing of truth, sharp;
                                    flies with its darkness
The wing of love flies too; but it is never alone   How
                            will you meet me?
Even abstract wings fly; slice us up with their light

XCIV

Infinity is liberation, or else it is nothing   Wouldn't we then
be slaves to infinity, subjected to freedom's constraint?

Already the intensity of light is plainly increasing; even if amplified by snowy surfaces
over the landscape of light's lowest level   The lowest souls are those of the tyrants,
Plato says; but I wonder about the hierarchies, if time's interlacing
is different, non-hierarchical   Angry cats get no sleep, you tell me

Then in the night we make love, shower together
I will go into the mountain of time, into its resonant, inner matter
It is not the light-sphere, which also resounds faintly   Signs of fire
                                        shine on the forehead

I touch the skin of night   I touch the resounding darkness
The impossible is completely abstract   Its love
But in the darkness your hands come to my face before you leave

Historical movements are not what we believe them to be
Then what are they? Movements within the larger brain?
No! I've said that the Great Man does not exist

Afterward I am inside the Empire   In its stasis   The dark eyes look at me
But I do not accept the empire   I accept no kingdom,
                        neither on heaven nor on earth,
                            nor any other place;
the thin flakes of birch-bark stir in the gray wind, invisibly   We are
                            the movements of history

The one thing that cannot change is zero   Infinity
is not stasis, rather the complete change of the all, all the time
Equally awful, equally unendurable, without love

XCV

God's universal economy touches us, with its laws, with its lack of
order
The black thrush hears us   Once I played the flute for it,
mimicked it, bewildered it   Until it resumed its song, sovereign, before
the sea   Where all the dead rose   I saw them coming; when I played
my own music   That
which has no alternatives   Taking in everything, everyone   In its attempt;
but it does not imitate
Order, too, in its birth is full of fear   So much pain

No syntax, no connections cease to exist   Once they have
existed   We will be in what does not exist   Endure its radiation
In the dream we are heroes; but I don't have much faith in that   It is a hallucinatory
world   Just as real   But no one knows before he has been tested
I envisioned torture, that it too would come here   Then I under-
stood: I myself stammered in the language of torture   Then I fell silent
Until the desperate babbling was revived   The string of language moves
out of the mouths of all, even the lost   The blocks of silence   The scream   Ut-
terly transparent   Silence is undefined   Thus it lacks
all autonomy   In the silence you can hear the faint sound of society, what
still exists   In all its cares, connections; its preparations

From Mexico came a bird, or a Bird-Angel, gleaming,
shimmering, metallic: violet, blue, green, a golden beak, wings   Com-
pletely unexpected   In the network: a map of Chiapas, news
of the continuing rebellion there, even after a year   I wonder how things are

in the Lacandonian Rainforest   The state of our planet: always crystallizing
For Swedenborg it was simpler   Every point of a human body,
a human brain, was influenced by a very large number of spirits, organized
in societies or associations   Music's movements in these associations,
18th-century, full of grace   Maybe also in Hell   Swedenborg seldom
bathed in his old age   I see the parchment of his face   Which words do we write
on the bodies of the stars   The wormwood stars   The celestial bodies

There is no exit   There is growing wakefulness   Growing sleep
The body of night is regenerated in symmetries   But we shall exist in growing
unknown structure, asymmetrical, falling, upward or downward, in the infinite
interstices between laws   As if we were the spirits, at
every point in the greater brain, or the body, with a new infinity
How does this help the dead? In no way   Maybe not the living either . . .

This is existence   Cities are pulverized; reconstructed
The obliterated tracks whisper   They are multiplied in stupendous music
The pressure of light goes inward   Imaginary worlds pass through one another
Not we   The friction, the resistance is real   In pain and in love

The ecstasy of silence   The ecstasy of dance   I read they should be the
extremes of different forms of time, being's and becoming's
respective timelessnesses   But I think: I have been in
their fusion   There's no difference there either
Maybe that's what is meant   The bird of prey's wing came swiftly, speckled
gray-brown   Then it was gone again   Fewer kinds of birds come to
the house this winter, I say   I miss the redpolls,
their graceful movements   I also miss the yellowhammers and the siskins

I just heard a crow   I think of the Gothic word *bigairdan*,
begird   With which garment, with which fence   And to serve
whom, what? We'll prepare a meal   Where do you find food for your life?
Fredman, too, girded himself   For a new ecstasy   Earth's music sounds
The brothers and sisters serve one another   When they do not kill one another

What can we give? Which value? As if there were anything but the one! The
white bands come like veils to the face that has dissolved   Come
closer, are   In the function of functions   Brimstone-yellow and violet light,
the faces of destruction are dark-eyed   The surfaces of the eyes almost wholly flat
How did life become possible? Again, again   The cries of the stars to one another
        almost
effaced   In complete brutality   The house of the stars bears emptiness
Fullness   Saturation   It must feel like hunger   Soon I will come
no further   What is, has already been   Time is, in its heightening

XCVI

Much is monstrous   But nothing is
more monstrous than man   Laws being broken through, their sounds,
their rhythms toward eternity, their fractal interference forms,
in the formats of expanding fans, trees, leaves
in the abyss of resonance, of reverberation . . .   What we are;
in our hopelessness, in our love   Against the
serial darkness, the form of pain, also in its raging fire of Hell . . .
Both darkness and total whiteness bear all colors . . .
Following catastrophes come awkward attempts at assistance   Also

fantastic ones   People who give their lives   Then worth goes from nothing
to infinity   Some even touch lepers   Then they are
stigmatized   I see a dark woman in a blue cloak, she sits in
onrushing darkness, moans a little, no one hears, she sits in the darkest
silence of her eyes   Don't know if I've seen her on the commuter train, in some
vision, in a picture . . .   I abuse the expression "don't know"
The abyss of the knowledge of nothing still touches us   How can I open myself?
The whiteness of the wind out the window   The cat who cautiously
steps from bare ground out across the snow   The withered oak leaf that twitches,
blowing across the snow   First I took it for a small animal
The impossible city on the mountain will also be destroyed   The color is
fiery-orange, red   Or colorless   As in a skyquake
Real angels are abstract, colorless, I read   Invisible
presence   It is we who are near   But laws, too, precipitate out of
the invisible   Infractions of them, in contempt of the human   What's broken
       through is
something else   What? As if there were some absolute difference   I
distrust all hypostases, the forms of revelation   I nag about
this   I want to be in the becoming, to be in its rhythms   The wind
carries all forms, blowing, streaming time   But we are also in being's
abyss   In the time of its emptiness   You went to school in the darkness of dawn, came
back in to say: Listen, the blackbird is singing! So we are
listening beings   But I did not hear it   I will not
add anything   The monsters move, in their dance

We are these rhythms, we are the beating of this wave, in toward the invisible shore
We are these trees, these birds   Strange creatures   In their sum
                              Everything we do to one another
bears this lightness . . .   We see their grace . . .   Impossibly . . .

XCVII

Sometimes it seems only the dead can say something about the living
Mercy is merciless, I hear myself say
We are, despite this, capable of laughing together . . .

Only in the highest music   Billie Holiday sings
This aching heart of mine is singing   The voice is light
completely surrounded by darkness   There is no end

XCVIII

The openings to the marvelous through music . . .   As if I'd been
afraid of the Paradise aspects for a long time   Straight through the music of
darkness   All those who resoundingly defend their lives   I myself
an awkward part of this music   That nonetheless streams from my body,
my hands   The resounding cry   In the stem of Charon's boat . . .

The Secret of Mozart's Brain reads the title of an article under
a portrait of the child Mozart, his fingers on the keyboard

The face is illuminated obliquely from the front or from above   The shadows
aren't right   He wears a wig, a red jacket   I'm reading about the left
frontal lobe's richer development in those who have absolute pitch
and wonder whether this actually pertains to Mozart . . .   That this then
should be connected with language   I'm thinking about tonal drift,
the variation in exact pitch since the 1700s, almost a half tone . . .
I have listened to Schoenberg's work for the organ, its wandering
all the more deeply into the labyrinth of mystery, alive, its prayer . . .
I hear the strata within the final note, its deep shaft into time,
vibrating   Again I feel deep satisfaction, although
this piece is usually dismissed as strange, formless, an anomaly . . .
We are the language we actually speak; we are in its endless song

There is music where doubt and pain come in on every
note, every fragment of sound . . .   As if just this were
the dawning of clarity, part of the human, in human relation
to God . . .   To hear this dynamic   To hear this as prayer, pain's
prayer, where there are never any guarantees   Play that way!

As if the sound of Mozart were almost the only one
not burnt to ash by the sound of pain, in its
wandering series . . .   Every day awkward attempts   Every day
the sound of blinding violence, in all its mirror-worlds
I move in traffic   Almost all people move
You who talk to me about sleep, telling me you sleep almost all the time,
but that you think, always think your own thoughts, not those of others, about
violence, narcissism, the vortex of rising need . . .

Yes, I say, and launch into a historical account
Later I wonder about this   Time cuts the conversation short

The enormous summary of many brains . . .   In a
societal form   Also for destruction   The collective
Mozart rushing toward the abyss, falling, like Don Giovanni
Viva la libertà! In which universal society does integration occur,
where science is insufficient   Because it, too, is an abyss
The rifts of war open everywhere anew, as with Hellish
awkwardness . . .   These formalizations are also altogether too rapid
in what is without mercy, or even without compassion   Hell
did not exist before creation   Nor shall it last eternally
Every form is the last   As if this were the annihilation point in
                                                    our brains . . .

The boldness, the brashness, which bursts the existing One,
and the man who falls through abysses, through eons, in the hierarchies
of dark mirrors, these, too, blinding with their darkness
How shall I explain to you the existence of evil?
Why it is repulsive to strike, wound, kill someone else—

Beneath the membrane of democracy the totalitarian grows, like a generalized
sore   Around all the walls is silence   Between the laws
new potentiality opens   Also new pain, new wounds   At an almost infinite distance:
the dance   That we carry   That carries us   I heard you, hear you

XCIX

In through the window, into the colors of the curtain
comes the winter light   Gray, muted   Far away you hear the tone,
the roar, from the city, from the activities of human beings   The angels have
their own peculiarities, flaws in their feathers   They too have their
colors of nothing, as they did for her, who loved pink
At her grave flowers grew   We placed stones on it
Human activities grow toward infinity   Finite in the infinite!
We shall dwell in sovereignty   There is no alternative
Not without denying what transcends   In the love star

C

Cities succeed one another   Of crystal   Of crystal
As if defined by an unknown algorithm   Which may be
wholly imaginary   The chaos of the world intensifies   I hear
the great tit; spring subdued, this first day of March   T walked with me
to the car, yesterday evening; we walked slowly   Wind   Stars
I pointed to a star shining brightly to the left of Orion,
said: That's got to be Mars, it has a pink sheen
T said something I couldn't make out, you mean Venus? I asked   Yes
But I'm quite sure her light is silver, I said   Thought about
Betelgeuse, unsure which star in Orion it was   Remembered
when I was a child, walking with Jan-Erik and Bengt-Arne to the top of
Gallows Hill to locate it   The name was very strange
I drove very quickly through the darkness   I phoned my mother, asked

about her stomach   No answer at my daughter's at first,
later she was home   The television displayed images of UN troops
retreating from Somalia, while the local militias again swarmed
the streets of Mogadishu, the small trucks mounted with low-
caliber cannon, or with heavy machine guns   The sneer on the soldiers'
faces   As if I were seeing the evacuation of the human
The famine and a part of the terror ceased for a short time   Anarchy's
iron mask momentarily visible   Living without laws is terrible   Like
living with angels   In one Inferno they punish the dead   Memories
move   Even in brains that are totally destroyed   *Hvaírneins stads,* I read
in the Gothic lexicon, the Place of a Skull, kraniou topos   Everyone's
brains re-created, exponentially   Crystal   Crystal   As if everything were
growing clarity, darkness   The brain in its flight, in a universal form
T and I conversed   Questions   Answers   The house of memories grew
        On the radio
a symphonic poem of Sibelius, *The Oceanides*   A kind of birth music
Before what? Reminiscent of the symphonic prelude to the concluding
sequence in Schoenberg's *Gurrelieder,* I said, and T nodded   On a paper
napkin he had written the year 1914, the year Sibelius composed the piece
The first great anarchy quickly developed   In one of my workbooks I had read
about the general, Giap, his remarks after the 1973 peace accords, where he thanked
all those who'd helped his people in the fight against the barbarians   T asked
        about Vietnam
I shook my head, told what I'd heard about a critical situation
quickly approaching, corruption, a regime more and more hollow, the police state
still in place, the population explosion   That a democratic alternative
capable of taking over when collapse came probably did not exist   We, too, are

the barbarians   Here, too, democracy erodes, ever since the movement toward equality
was broken, was repulsed—

CI

What is being prepared? Which birth is coming   Which
child, eternally God? The birth comes monstrously
The large numbers grow   As if they had their own special laws
There shall be new forms of time   Death's time   The time of the living
All creation occurs so slowly   Quick as a flash   Then the created
see us   By which time we are in the underworld, its resonant heavens

But sometimes I also speak with the living   The Books of the Thorn Rose go on
being written   Contact is light, light; completely serious

Mozart comes decked out, mimetically, as Harlequin, Pierrot . . .
But he imitates no one; he is completely himself   His own
music sounds, a violin part   What remains after the devastation

The living touch me, delicate skin covering their crania, their bones
Alone, desolate, they walk among the dead, without their families
The mimetic eye sees them   We look into that eye, nearly petrified

CII

In the city of the brain every landscape exists   Even Hell and
Paradise   And Purgatory   Each landscape where we are not   And that
is not   This is strangely familiar   I thought: The resurrection
of all bodies must be a new creation, just as complete
as the old one   Perhaps a different light shines on it, but I
don't really understand why   We are in this creation

Is it possible to enter the music of putrefaction
without rotting? As if in an inviolable light   While everything says
in reality I am touched   Thus I must be inside
this ripeness, though I've always despised all ripeness   Its sweetness

The fire burning, invisible . . .   Even in the transparent
membranes, permeable, to infinity, eternity's
membrane, a quotation? Of what? This, too, is the conflagration
We don't always know where impulses come from   In the series of
connected brains   Time is born out of us, as our child, of infinity

Can I describe this? Yes, I can   But I don't know how
What exists exists only afterward   I enter
the dark gateway, between labia of black stone, shimmering
purple   The tracks of the sun move inside   The diamond oar
The sea-space is enormous   The arms of its currents move galactically
The smile is coming   Isn't this far too large? Yes! No!

In a flash imaginations extend into the real   We are
beyond all controls   The societal images,
in the media, in the information nets, full of manipulation, intentions,
their own inner blindings   I suddenly understand Plato,
his dream of a world beyond mirages, which renders even them
entirely derivative, but he seems not to have understood it was
a solitary world, existing solely in the transcendence within a single person,
and that they cannot be converted into laws . . .   Diotima
was not reality for him, as she may have been for Hölderlin,
even though she had children, a spouse . . .   The rain has now changed to snow
I listen to the sound of spring birds   Has the great tit's dialect changed?
Our language is partly a bird language   We're learning continually

CIII

Dear little mommy in the mother tree   You are in its burning sound
To which leaves do I listen? To which shell in the ear?
Now I hear your fear   You shall be in the Mozart tree
Whose sound deepens   It will carry across the deep sea
The city by the sea is wrapped in smoke   The light on the sea
The deep tree of the ocean   I stand beside its trunk, look into its crown

People are in their motions   In the big hospital at night
I saw people's lives, their saved lives, saw intense attempts
at life   Saw one person lying on his side, the skin under his eyes
purple   Tubes   Apparatus   My mother lay with her head just visible

above the blanket, some gray, some yellow in her face   But we spoke
with each other   I walked out into the darkness   The city with its lights lay below
Then the rain came   I read about the development of science, its invisible

brotherhoods

Sisters seemed wholly excluded   Earlier in the day I had
read the last canto of The Inferno   Satan's six-winged mill drove the wind forth
The way back, beyond the point of utmost weight, narrow, steep, a small stream
In The Inferno there was, as I thought, no music   Yet the dominating
sound was of compassion, even if interwoven with loathing, hate   The verse
carries the music, the central sound   The voice is carried to her, who listens
Love's little wind moves   Flowers already rise from the soil, colored

arrows

Infractions from below, in the continual geometry   Down toward
point zero, in the unending movement   I knew it
almost from the first, through dreams, in which I was crushed
between piston strokes of infinities   *But this is no machine*
In mathematics there is no friction, no work
is performed   What made my body shake was its own work
But life is not work, perhaps not even the fight against death is
The voice sings   What sings through it is another voice
We are the attempt at greater song   This too breaks the geometry
We cannot control the measurements of earth   We are the greater earth

In the second canto of The Purgatorio comes music, the song of the souls,
then Casella, who sings of the love that speaks to a person
in his mind   And no one listens to anything but that   The sound of
The Inferno entirely gone   The weeping, the lament, Nimrod's horn, the frog mouths

chattering in the cold, the huge drum of a stomach, when someone kicks it
A world of sound, no music   *There is no music without love*
But there is also recursion, where love becomes Hell's
There is music in the modern Inferno   I myself have heard it
Genocide's planets are rising   We are under the dark star

In the investigative light   Freedom's light, that opened up over
the city   Where I never expected it   Where until now I have not seen
the topography clearly   From the ridge I see the fault line in the distance,
the scarp toward the sea   In the distance I also see the sea's movements
Clouds cross over the ridge, in the northwestern sky's heavenly sheen   The wind
has bent the treetops   Today snow is falling, as I have not seen it
since childhood   Movement tentatively begins within each city, each place

There beyond the houses is the sea   Threatened now by freshwater streams
from Europe's winter floods   But I cannot remember
a time without threat   Mustard gas   Mine explosions
The black, stinking water of Nissan   The form of the name in
Old Swedish was Niz, derivation uncertain   Outside here the Battle of Nissan
    took place
in 1062   A Danish nobleman, Sven Estridsen, rose up
against the Norwegian king, Harald Hårdråde, but was defeated here
in a huge battle at sea   In *Nizarvisur* by Steinn Herdisarson
Harald had 150 ships and Sven 300   Who saw this from the ridges?
What fires burned atop the fault scarps? The mathematical
conflagration was lit   From the height I searched for Betelgeuse,
where we stood together, almost children, in a battle we did not yet know

Fragility of the waters, beneath the cities   Gliding, vibrating
Hatred rising, terror   Human value violated
Fragments of music come, as in an unconscious state, an ignorance of
sorrow, before it rises, burning   In the darkly dissolved faces
People still talk to one another as if human value were possible
Even though we know it is immortal   Thus beyond human beings

CIV

I lay a light stone on my father's grave, a gray stone
on the gray stone   Hadn't planned to, it just happened
Then I think: Now you have made him a Jew   But then I realize
that this is about one kind of infinity, in the series of infinities
On Gallows Hill the brimstone butterfly flutters, the jay is in the tree
In the hospital my mother tells me I have been to Väderön, which we can see
in the distance   Veils of mist at the foot of Kullaberg   But even the smaller islands
near Väderön are visible across the sea   Then I remember   How water from the waves
beat into the open boat   Also remember seeing the horn of a narwhal in Torekov

Mozart in the first brain; in the resounding second: music
We are in the excluded third, impossibly, in the counterpart, its
constant alteration, as in all other brains   We are a small part
of it   So music touches us, all music, past and future
As if we were in the focus of love itself, its one and only point
I listen to all the voices, I hear their care, their rage   Hear all
the instruments, in all their dimensions   Hear the darkness of the sound

The fine weave of light moves upward, with its voices   Until even
the earth sings, from its depths   My lips move in the fugue, in dissonance
In my deep smile   As if all pain, all joy, simply existed
Children move restlessly   The voices of the old speak of loneliness, abandonment

Today I bring my mother home   As if she were a child
In this I feel very childish myself   Yesterday I spoke with M,
B's rescuing angel   She talked about having spent the day
in Laxvik, where she'd seen the eider ducks coming, how they rose like smoke
down toward the mouth of Lagan, over the long sandy beach
I sensed early spring, the sea, gray, gray-green   The visions of birds
she and B had together, that attentiveness   As when B listened to
music, an unceasing astonishment   It will soon be two years since he died

The tension between gnosis and the absence of knowledge, inside me   That the
one thing that holds is what prevails through gnostic arrogance
I've understood this can also exist in the imageless
That arrogance, knowledge, its absence, all love, its absence, take
all forms   Here I can sense the disruptions in language   The invisible obstacles
pushing upward, crystal forms in the interior, those once crushed by song—
Will the song return, again, again   I really cannot know that   I re-
peat this, over and over again   A nag warbler   But also like the blackcap . . .

CV

Not-Orpheus is singing   He sings his nothing   He sings his night
He sings all the names   The name of nothing   The only name   Since

long ago   He didn't know it   And knew it in his night
All things sing   All names sing   Every tonal difference, every
sound   All music in its destruction   In its sublation   Toward which point?
The mountain of nothing hovers   Before it crushes us   With its night   With its song

In the evening I walked through town with you, Dearest, along the river
A clear cold spring evening, the half-moon shone   As if walking in a foreign city
Though I recognized parts of it   You said it was almost like
walking in Prague, where we would have been if my mother hadn't fallen ill
When we stood by one corner of the Hotel Svea, where I played in a dance band
   in 1957,
the huge flock of jackdaws, in the trees by the bastion near the castle, flew
out over the river, in micropolyphonic conversation   As in a piece by Ligeti
That night I dreamed I crossed a bridge spanning the river, now very broad
The long bridge was swaying, huge ocean swells entering the river from the sea
I walked with a girl, kissed her on the mouth, on the opposite bank
In the morning you came into my bed, Dear, we slinked like teenagers, so my
            mother wouldn't hear us,
where she slept, in the room outside ours   She's already much better
I look at my face in the bathroom mirror   Will I manage to go out into the Brain

Trucks pass   Traffic goes on, in the great exchange of goods
Gulls, trees, people   The degree of virtuality in different goods, the phantasms
also in what we eat, conceptions of origin, contents, effects
Fear   Cultivated tastes   We are in the immediacy of memory   Only in a flash of
astonishment can memory be broken   But even lightning is informed   I look at the
            magical

diagrams of Giordano Bruno, read his texts   See that all this is exactly

as in

Jung, fundamental magical forms, for guiding the divine,

the unknown within the soul   Also the similarity with tantric forms   Yes, that's

how it is,

I think, both Freud and Jung are magicians, the difference in rationality is

only marginal, Jung's a little older, Freud's more modern, a continuation of

Descartes, developed later in Spinoza's pneumatic model for the passions,

and yet both are found, subsumed in Bruno's love-flow, the lineage backward,

the tantric flow, also Plato's Diotima, her flow . . .

Hölderlin saw the stream of people in dark water, streaming over

the ledges in the human-geological world, the levels of the abyss, Para-

dise's various degrees of stasis

What use can I make of these magical forms? I'm no magician   And yet

I acknowledge their power, also within my self   If they prevail, sovereignty

is crushed   *Libero arbitrio*   There the forms also break down

The stream of love breaks down   Fluid lightning   The flash of vibrating being

But also the flash of darkness   The light of Beatrice's eyes, their lightning flash   How

am I to understand this? How to understand unknowing   That I do not!

CVI

Which is the time of music? I know I exist inside it, liberated

As if this were the core: the dance, the throat, the instruments

Listening, I play   Unknown music grows out of the instrument
Time grows out of me   All the more clearly, out toward the outermost tips
    of the galaxies
I am a comet, I imagined when I was little, dashing
around the schoolyard, arms outspread behind me like wings . . .

Stalin, too, loved Mozart   Thus even these forms are
completely empty   Interpretations know no limits
Nor shall we have any guarantees   Art is
not an insurance company, not a question of trust, and thus not politics
Disorder is complete   In Dante I find the word *modern*

The deep architecture of heaven, in its turnings   In music
I hear its deep mysteriousness   I hear its openness
The birds, in their movements over the planet's surface   I see the cranes,
on the banks of Ljusnan, on the field of brown earth, between
flat patches of snow   The water dark, streaming   Heaven's abyss
moves   The fragile, stinging stars rise   How do we
touch one another's souls   In severity's order   In what can only be grace

The skinny woman of about 50, in the May Day demonstration,
who said, never again would she vote for the Social Democrats
All over her face and body she bore the mark of someone betrayed
Who speaks now for the lowest? And in which language?

Karl is dying now   M was there yesterday, to help out with
the shelves for the LPs   Karl lay in bed the whole time, did not want

to or could hardly speak, but was there mentally   Maybe it's
the morphine, I said, that's making it hard to focus, intellectually
I got the impression, said M, that Karl has now decided
it is time   I recall the severity in Karl's face, the enormous
seriousness, the first time I was up at the offices of *Aftonbladet,*
in 1967, with the poem "To the National Liberation Front of South Vietnam";
he read it in my presence   His probing examination, his concentration
How I wondered if it would hold up   In the end almost
nothing does   Except for what exists in the time that is of eternity

The music deeper and deeper toward darkness   The prelude to Siegfried,
the tubas, the basses   Again in Mahler, Scelsi   How this touches
Europe, invoked also in Dante, in The Paradiso   The third
age will come, according to Joachim de Fiore   But this, too,
will suffer decadence, before perfection in the Last Judgment   Here
all the ages move more rapidly, everything blended, confused   Realms
succeed one another   Within each human being his time   The vector cloud of times
moves, in the stream of people   Under the mountain of the heart hubris grows

CVII

Karl Vennberg

Karl is dead   He was a man without guile   Blinding
white, with snow, the May morning the day he died
The light yellow-green of small birch leaves shimmering under
that white   Snow over everything   I had a thought, all day long,

that maybe Karl was dying   Late in the evening the message came
I called B   When I told her she wept   Later on my tears came

CVIII

I hear my father saying: Are you stark-raving mad? The rapidly outdated
language moves like snowflakes through my memory   The dead do not rest
They walk through the world, we don't need to call to them   They are
their own interpretation   They, too, exist in what's foreign   We are parts of language

We cannot take anything back   Can we stop short of the abyss?
We fall deeper and deeper, glass-clear, as if in justice to clarity
But nothing is clear   Intuitions come hovering, scarcely distinguishable
forms in nothing, like ice-profiles in water, the dragonfly's vanishing
pairs of wings   The small mountain ashes' new leaf bouquets emerge, into nothing

Becoming in annihilation   A slightly varied formulation
of Hölderlin's thought   Disappearing far out on one of
the tangents of glass   While the hypersphere grows and grows
I hear impersonal music, no human's music
Again I'm very scared   What do I dare? What don't I?
What kinds of becoming   The existing annihilations rampage all around us
In which do we take part   Breaking out into total answerability

But I don't accept this   I pluck off the red beetles
that are chewing up the fritillarias   One of the cowslips in the grass
has red flowers   You say it was there last year as well   We

see society move, just under the skin   The enormous forces
In growing industrial amplifications   Resonances   Shaking
the ground, the hills, all the bridges, all the connecting strings   Wave connections
All projectiles moving toward the transparency of the luminous skull . . .

The personal brain   The one that grows through human interaction,
and through the interaction of humans with all other beings and entities
Growing, beyond time, like mountain ridges   Which are completely contingent

Poverty's brain   The one that never got to grow out
to its full potential   Or one that was damaged in
some other way   How the brain is in its completeness, its full worth
Even the angelic hierarchies are equalized, as in a mystical blossoming

CIX

In another room the world is coming to an end   At a distance clear as glass
people are annihilated; or are destroyed from within by murder
I have to act now! Crush this house that grows, that en-
velops the larger house   In the house of the stars of fugitive crystal
I don't want to take part in the annihilation   The impossible only grows
But this cannot be solved even in the underworld of paradoxes . . .

Deeper and deeper into God as matter   Music moves across the obscure
Music in its own dark clarity   *There* is all tenderness, and all joy
Nowhere   Nothing   Feeling moves naked, without attributes   Waiting
But tears come when I least expect them and I am happy

The right to say no is the basis of democracy   But only within the matrix of
a deeper yes   That which lies beyond each acceptance
of power imposed from outside   I look at the light of early summer, drink
its milk   The leaves of the aspen come now too, a light brownish yellow
On the new plum tree are also some small, very small flower buds . . .

And if this larger yes is death   The tree in its dizzying flight
We are always the answer   We don't always know who is asking the questions

I go up on the mountain   On the path I look at a crumbling
conifer false morel and at small black morels, *Morchella elata*,
two of them, one still intact   From the crest I look out over the landscape,
at patches of lake, forest-clad ridges, suburbs, under veils
of haze, under the sun as it descends   The air full of the scents
of flowers and new leaves on the trees   We visited
G in the hospital, in the thoracic clinic, after he'd had a lung removed
He looked better than I thought he would, wanted to hear about Karl's funeral,
so we told him   About the prayer that somehow hovered over the coffin
I think about the concept of God as Nothing, Nowhere   Over
this darkness   Over the time of Nothing   Where is Karl now, G asked, as he
coughed and became very tired   He wanted us to see the Atlas Moth
in the Butterfly House in Haga Park   B has already written about that, I said . . .

CX

Petrifaction's gaze? Or mental automata? The passageway
between, between interstices between all things   What we cannot see
even as possibility   What by definition belongs to the impossible
This too grows from the ashes in iron vessels
What constitutes the human may still be only in its beginning

In the flowing heavenly archives   Of lead   In jubilation-torment
Hephaistos touched the stream of Okeanos, when he fashioned
the automata, tripods with wheels, serving
the gods   Also figures of girls made of gold, who spoke

Who was Mozart? Who is he, in his becoming   Deeper and deeper
clarity, downward   Music sounds in the growing silence, all the more
clearly, farther and farther down   We stand near the flowing ocean, its
silence   As if a new birth were to come   But we do not know if it will

The picture of Kolchak's soldiers, killed by firing squad, Omsk, 1919
One of the century's piles of corpses, later generalized   The same kind
of order of accessions   The variants of permanent murder are but a single one
The dead lie stacked, like firewood; separate fruits of the tree

Even in Mozart there's a binding to the nation, to what is German . . .
He says it himself, but transcends it in the music, which
penetrates all realms   It is the same in
Hölderlin, but more dangerous there, because he links the nation
with death   Death is present all the time

Personal death comes　It moves like faces
under water, small pains, fear　I have been there before
Childish fear, suffocation　The overwhelming darkness
I was with my father and my mother, but they could not help me . . .

Sound develops, in its complete humanness　Alive,
I touch you　Alive, you touch me　We still touch each other
I hear the wind in the trees　A warm wind　It is the wind of summer
Where the wind blows no one knows　It is no one's wind　No one's summer
The wind blows for all the dead　Also for the living, cast like seeds
Now　Now I deliver myself up　May the wind blow where it will　Also to you
I know that I love you　I feel that you love me　I stroke your hair

CXI

Ormöga, 1995

Swallows' wings out the window, when they fly up to the nest
Their light undersides　A patch of space over one of earth's landscapes
Below it is limestone, with its other space, downward
Behind me, hidden, to the back of my head, is the sea

The weave of living things, tighter and tighter　We look at
the spotted-flycatcher nestling, its round eyes, streaked head,
in half of a swallow's nest under the eaves, its tail sticks out outside

The darkness of the wings approaches   From all directions   Whirling
How shall I make anything out in this surging noise? Who
will be gathered up? Which message, to whom?

The flock of starlings comes flying, making tiny sounds   The darker
parents feed the lighter chicks   When the wind blows
from the northeast, the house is leeward of the grove   From there you can hear
    the cuckoo
The wind stirs up waves in the sea of grass, exposing its different colors
All the different forms of the grass spikes   Their aspects scatter the light

Today I will go and see the dead woman   I hear her voice
all the time, just as it spoke to me, through all the years
In her voice was honesty, knowledge   Never anything false
Nothing can take that away   It is perpetuated

CXII

                        Will my time suffice? For which
song, for which translation   We will all be carried over   With which ferry?
We emerge, liberated, from matter   That's how we create its freedom
We are in many worlds simultaneously   We are also in many brains . . .

We walk together through meadows of orchids; all the thousands
of flowers, all the night-scented orchids, the smaller, white, and the larger
yellowish green; all the fragrant orchids, their different colors, purple

to light creamy violet, a few disparate ones entirely white
The fly orchids, their purple-brown, insect-shaped flowers, these too
in different colors, degrees of lightness   The purple-lilac torches of the early
        marsh orchids
The burnt orchids, with their dark hoods   We walk there, as in the meadows of Hades,
but in the land of the living   We see the buzzard and the heron   The curlew circles
around us, crying warning   The redshank chick cries kleep-kleep, from the fence-
post toward the sea   When we get to the sea we see a flotilla of swans,
in the little bay to the north, on the stones in the distance cormorants sit

To whom does my brain belong? With what can I or you resist? Within me disorder
While my brain seeks its order, at almost any price . . .

All of us return to the dead   Now we visit their graves together
Sometimes I am alone   When I speak with the dead I am always alone
I speak with the dead in the language of the dead   I also speak with birds
The feelings are identical   But the dead can no longer think new thoughts . . .

CXIII

The delicate light of the night-scented orchids on the heath, late evening sun
We walk in their scent   We drop to our knees to inhale
the musk orchid, its special fragrance   It smells like honey,
you say   You prick your hand on a dwarf thistle   No, I
say, it smells different, a bit strange   We are not strangers here

Under the wall's whitewash is putrefaction's image   A mother
We are informed by the absence of knowledge   Does a third form exist?

                                        Mozart's final hour,
the instruments are smashed, in some preformative statements   Word
propositions, below shrilling flutes, the larger stringed instrument's
multitude of voices   And the Muse for me invents, for me in her
presence, with a new shimmering, a turn for the dance of my foot . . .

What kind of society is coming? And to which society are we the increment?
I look at the swallows and the swifts, their different geometries . . .
I look at the wild roses in their different colors, pure white to
pink, the new flowers of the pink ones have a tinge of yellow
I brought you one of them   The bird in the thicket cried warning   On the road
I ran over a viper, which we looked at later, it was beautiful
In each person a society is built   Different societies, their points of conflict,
areas of confrontation   This is Kypris's tract   No one else has rights here
No one has the right to usurp the rights of others   This defines society

CXIV

How is the tower of memory now built? Mnemosyne's city a growing labyrinth
A swift flies under the metal roof tile of the dormer facing
the heath   Out there is the sea, with its faraway gaze   Ormöga, *Snake Eye*, is inland
Farthest out on the spit we saw avocets, again, grubbing in the mire
with their upcurved beaks   Slender birds, fantastic in their beauty

In horizontal sunlight, a black swan swims alone
among blinding white ones   It is somewhat smaller,
with a narrower, slightly longer neck, its red beak shining   Always
moving toward the white swans, which swim away
The sea is very calm, beneath the white moon   The redshank
flies complaining   With friends we walk across the heath by the shore
Patches of night-scented orchids shine   We discuss *Convivio*, the Banquet,
a kind of summation, a kind of philosophical commentary on poetry, concretely
executed, the book unfinished   I think about Dante's politics, his acceptance
of the highest office, in Florence of the democratic principle,
how at this time he shared responsibility for Cavalcanti's banishment,
how later he lost everything   During one period of time concrete hopes for
universal empire, before these too were lost, in practical terms
I wonder if I would have said to him, too, he was already dead
Dew falls on the grass   Cavalcanti virtually said this   I think about
my own politics   How I entered the tower of nothing   Perhaps there's no
way out of nothing   Thorn roses bloom all the time, these short weeks
we are here, almost over   The wine we drink is La Diva, from the valley of Paradise
Finally we hear news from Srebrenica, the enclave has fallen,
tens of thousands of people stream out into the landscape, in headlong flight

There are people who won't even accept the justice of the underworld
The dead shall be driven from their graves   This is a complete hunger
The moonlight's reflection in the sea shines through the pine grove; mystical silver light
There is no national liberation   Perhaps neither is there universal
The empire of love exists only between individuals, in its impersonal power
And the integral? It only moves under its blinding darkness, its stars

In the summer night only one single star shines   We hear the corncrake;
from the grove with the thorny thicket a repeated shriek, maybe an owl chick?

In which direction does the movement go   *Logos*—answers, responses, questions—has
no direction, in its complete intellect   Love has no logos . . .

CXV

Radical magnification   Pain's needle removes almost everything
Radical diminution   We are also in the annihilation that is joy's
All the faces see   With their abysses of eyes, non-reflective

Three springs arise from the alvar, like eyes   I immerse my hand
to where the flow originates, from below, from the crack in the limestone
The water quite cold   Around my hand I feel the flow's
revolving motion   As if it were a woman's sex, transparent, pulsating
Around the wellsprings butterworts grow, their light-green, sticky leaves,
some with black insects   A marsh helleborine stands alone, beautiful
This one lighter than those on Gotland, which grew around the sand marsh on
Sudret, the pale purple of the sepals with small streaks of green
We wash our faces in the clear water   Blue libellulas fly
We look at the runestones near Sandby church, and at the snakeheads where
the gables peak on the old barns   The lacertines move in the stone
Above them is a sun-sign   At night a line of thunderstorms approaches, with its
                                                            own world of signs
We saw pictures of multitudes of refugees from Srebrenica, when we re-
turned from the seashore; I finished reading the book about Dante   He never gave up

the concept of universal empire   He was within his vision
In Bosnia universal power has been degraded, the power that should be universal
is not, is nothing but the shadows of the minor empires   In what is half-
way invisible   The suffering is real   The moral degradation is real
Some people help   Impotence's reflections also destroy people
I shower in the glow of lightning, because I got tired of waiting   Next comes
the light through shut eyelids, with its fiery sheen, before I too fall asleep

Those who commit genocide are also real   We see them embrace one another   It is
entirely repulsive   I too shall enter the war of shadows
Who has once made war can never forget it   With my body's soul
I touched what is repulsive; I closely searched the turning, the transformation of
the signs in the heavens, in the universal war   The rock-roses shine yellow
    on the Alvar,
and also here, by the house, in the grass   Here, where I've set up my tower
Against the snake's gaze   The swallow chicks also look at me here, from their nest
I hear them now, in the quiet   Through the open window came the scent of the sea
We are in the universal brain; parts of it   Parts of its inner annihi-
                                   lations
The inner reflections blot one another out   We shall be there, as in a nest

CXVI

                The wind of the darkness of the sea   In Mozart's
third brain music continues   Within its transparent niche-work   But we
are not concealed   We are everywhere the same   All people are particular

No one is nearer   More remote   War's thunderbolt shoots straight through
    the brain where-
ever we happen to be   We are all neighbors   In this growing connection
Will it also become a growing emptiness   A human vacuum that is
                                     almost continual
genocide   The emptying continues   We are the mirror of this poverty
The curlews fly together, with short, drilling sounds, over the field

CXVII

Vänneböke, 1995

If we ourselves do not become instruments; flutes harshly ringing
In so doing we ourselves become inhuman; the guilt we take on
for the most part repressed; the murder invisible, concealed; and comparing
magnitudes will not do   We are always in the morally repugnant

The journey goes simultaneously toward the center and the extreme
of the periphery, and toward the impossible third term   The imaginary
spaces look at us, with the paradox of their eyes   The
real eyes also look at us, from the death-enclaves, as if they were
within ourselves   All spokesmen   All intercessors   Can I
accept someone other than she who is disinterested? Who sees us
with her darkness   Who only becomes possible straight through central Hell
I am in all this, as if I were dead   In my revelations   In the light of my vision

I will lose all controls   Problems, as posed, hunt me down
I am their problem   I seek no solutions   They seek me out
Toward which despair? I move the dance of my foot   In blinding joy

I drive alone to my aged mother   The large lines of the landscape   The ridges
The sea   The soft hills with Bronze Age graves   The immense light
The acute sense of being at home   Why should I be anywhere else
This is extremely suspect   I find my mother completely recovered, after
the operation, her small body suits her   What do we talk about   The
usual, not much   But we are there in existence, for each other   A little
while longer   When I drive back to the woods at dusk my eyes strain
                                                    for animals   None
come; the road moves softly   I move between different landscapes

Also in these I shall find my extremity   The Paradise of the limestone heath, with
all the orchids, in the flatland of Hades   As if I saw two burning houses, a single
simultaneous offering   The double pride of the angels, those in Heaven and
        those in Hell,
also touches me   I will be in the center   That which is everywhere

The shallows shine with their different colors, green, brown, gray-black
In Torekov I touch the western sea   On the shore outside Ormöga
I touched the eastern sea   As if in that way I drew a huge arc across
the land   We enclosed by it   An endless fermata   So the sound arises

CXVIII

The first of the Greek thinkers who localized perception and thought
in the brain seems to have been Alkmaion of Croton, one of the Pythagoreans . . .
How do we attain knowledge? As if music penetrated deeper and deeper   In its
                                                 greater and greater simplicity

The crowns are built, in their topological forms, mirrored or
not mirrored, imaginary or real, the forms of pain, the forms
of joy   Dance   The links between them   Whether continual or discrete
For a brief moment we cannot know   In this tension we exist
Whether living or dead   Whether form or impossible form
Harmony tenses   Then spreads out its shimmering fan-wing
Widening its darkness, its luminous pain   Then it touches me

We are also in the worlds of putrefaction   There is no peace there
The victims have the right to bear arms   Whosoever they are   Almost regardless
        of the price
Grace can be won with the atom bomb, Ekelöf wrote, in scorn . . .

One can begin anywhere at all   Accessibility is
hyper-reactive, is touched by infinity's orders
You touch me, with your sensitivity   I am touched, answer

Your sister was on television, from Tuzla   She described
how they took care of the refugees from Srebrenica, her
face severe, somewhat tense   I felt tears come

Cepa has fallen   Karadzic and Mladic are indicted in The Hague
for genocide and crimes against humanity   This is right

The intensity of infinities grows   The intensity of Hell
Of Paradise   As if they were worlds with no connection to one another
And yet perfect mirrors   The souls of the foreigner and the enemy
look into the souls of the foreigner and the enemy   An infinite number of worlds
I do not accept this   Even if the worlds have
infinitely small dimensions, attaining reality only in the continuum   Its
labyrinth   We are real in another way   How
can I get to the bottom of this   I cannot   There is no bottom

CXIX

Reduction to derivative structures? No! They are new parts
of the universe   Systems of relations; sounding; or not
sounding   Then we hear their silence   Because we ourselves consist of sound
Theories are coming   Like shadow forms out of music   Become their own
kind of music, transforming us completely, emerging from within themselves
as in continual rebirth   Then they lie crushed
under the trees   We, crushed   We will never be restored
For there is never anything to return to   What exists is
the joy of new form   We see that in every child   Also in every new
thought, even if it belongs to Hades   The boat sets out   The sail is set
A red spritsail   On the gray islets lay a clump of heavy oil, big
                                        as the head of a calf
Now all that was very long ago   For some time we've been very old children—

You enter, or you do not enter   It's hard
to know in advance   And you're already inside,
as if you didn't know it   Different for every
person   For every person perhaps an infinite number
of entrances   Or exits   The diamond gate   The soft
rock   Black   The upright mouth, completely
soft   The number one   The number zero   Infinity is built
from there   If it's not there beforehand   There are damaged
numbers, impossible in every kind of logic   But the brain is not logical
The brain consists of sound, objectified or not objectified

Mozart's brain, already closed, among those already dead   Thus it is
complete sound, unfinished, because it lives in us,
even if we are annihilated, already non-existent   It is independent
of his soul, even if it should exist, in some realm of eternity
Because construction still goes on   The towers are built higher and higher
The small huts   The trees   The labyrinths   The bog where cloudberries
grow, and which we pick, in a moment of peace, between
conflicts   The sun   The smell of the swamp   Bog asphodel and cross-leaved heath
Leaves of bog myrtle that I take in my hand and crumble between my fingers, their
fragrance   The lake's dark water that softly surrounds us   Where you bore
the child, the one we lost   We are together, repeatedly, repeatedly
Increasing hunger   It is never stilled   It exists in its consummate peace

CXX

I am not in the world of intention   The interior, balancing brain
has other goals, beyond reduction, necessary for
all understanding   The world of *charis*, the world of grace, this too
in its mercilessness   Yes, I read you, your book, leafing through
the pages of your invisibility   The brain grows out of eternity, as something
that has never existed before   But this also applies to the brain of darkness

I hear your light voice, your love   Now the sun shines in on me, where
I sit writing   Now it's time for packing and cleaning   This time I do them
alone, since you have an urgent task to attend to   Between us music's deep
harmony   I shall never forget this   Together we are music

Now I will phone you   I think: Afterward I have something to finish
Nothing is determined by intention   This is an objective property of time
Your love does not seek its own   I seek you out, that which is your love

CXXI

At every point new dimensions open, and with them
new connections   What kinds of connections? Touch
may not be the only one   Action-at-a-distance? Other kinds of messengers?
But the gospel may be completely dark   Straight through the world of genocide

Blossoming eons   In the night and the stillness over the lake stars were blazing
In the morning I heard a loon's cry   Soft, soft   The surface of the water like
silk, shimmering   I spend the night with friends, before I continue on my way

CXXII

Ethnic cleansers confront ethnic cleansers   The sign of
genocide appears, again and again, between clouds   Mozart
wrote war music for the siege of Belgrade, stooping down
to imperial power   *Viva la libertà!* I shall listen to human music,
at almost any price   Also to the song of wrath   The town of Otočac was bombarded,
I read in the paper the other day, where one night Gunnar Ekelöf
heard gypsy music, on his human journey, without power . . .

Now I hear the death song   Go down, to the great heaven of the underworld—
I am finally learning, in broad strokes, the architecture of the brain
Medulla   Pons   Midbrain   Hypothalamus, with
the pituitary, on its stalk   I look things up in books, in order to learn
more   Everywhere incomplete pictures   The pineal, resting on the corpora
quadrigemina   Thalamus   Fornix, passing into the hippocampus,
with its gyrus   Amygdala   The cerebellum with its tree of life   Archi-
cortex   Corpus callosum   Neocortex, the cerebrum's bark,
its enormous sail, in infinity's wind   Eyes   Inner ear   All the
membranes, vessels, ventricles, glands that produce cerebral fluid inside there . . .

A survivor from Srebrenica   Smail Hodzic, 63 years old,
tells his story   More than 2,000 of the males were lined up in front of machine guns
and shot   A man falls over him, dead; some hours later he can
crawl away over more than 200 dead bodies into the woods
This is Riga 1941   Or White Russia, or the Ukraine   It is eastern Cambodia
in June 1978   Turkey 1915   Croatia, also 1941   The catalogue is
unfinished   It falls into its own deep logos   I listen to Schoenberg's
A Survivor from Warsaw   Falling into the abyss of art   You see
my contorted face   Secure as we are   At this distance
You walk by, saying that I shouldn't make such horrible faces   You do not see
inside me, you don't hear the music   The chorus sings, SH'MA YISROEL   What
    do people
in Bosnia sing? What did they sing in Cambodia? In which silence
The Gypsies sing, *Dsha tele*, go down   Nordic countries in the 16th century   Nation-
states being born   I do not want to be in the national   Nor in the Empire
I want to be in the excluded third term, but it's impossible   Shards
of the laws lie shimmering on the ground, opalescent   Look into them   Look into
                                      the abyss
The mountain of its point, of nothing, lays a claim on love . . .   Its something

CXXIII

T played a fugue for the left hand by Ponce, a Mexican composer
The sound hovered, lifted off   As if for a moment the brain's clarity opened
to its full extent   Its capacity is enormous   The grand piano's red-brown wood
    trembled

CXXIV

Go into the throbbing brain of crystal   Red to light-red   As if it were
death   I am Not-Orpheus; I play a flute of crystal
I walk inside the brain's underworld   It grows all around me

I stand at the seashore   I hear the voices of thousands of small waves   Out there
a storm is brewing, a small, white point   Growing toward infinity
I am inside it   Below me grows the infinite brain   Then it is
infinitely small, darkness's point   A star; in a universe of crystal
Whom do I meet inside there   Who follows me   I follow your soft voice
        Farther and
farther in, darker and darker   Through the windows of the eyes the world is
        visible   In its
overwhelming abundance   Through all the senses   In the underworld
        the doomed sing,
for us, for one another   Also with the sound of genocide   That which can only
be conquered by life   Also in those who walk straight into death . . .   There is
nothing else   An old woman, in one of the zones contaminated by
Chernobyl, plays with her grandchild, says: We will all die, no one knows
when   She does not know   The child does not know   Nor do I know

When the gates of crystal open   The crystal cranium opens
When I am in its breathing   When this openness breathes in me
In all the demon-colors   In its clarity, its light   Even in-
to the uttermost darkness   Straight through the projections of fear
Straight through love   Straight through hate   All combinations

are possible   Straight through all skin, all tissue   To the burning
form, the form of all forms   Completely dark   Complete love

The brain rests in its darkness   The mute light of pain   The sharp
light of pain   One summer's day in September I walk to Lövholmen   On
Kofsan I stop and look at the stalks of henbane, the rows of its seed vessels
already brown   Then I also see new shoots, their dusky yellow flowers
speckled violet around violet centers   In a damaged elm
I see a mourning cloak, first it flutters among the still-green leaves, then sits
on the trunk, moves its wings, as if violently breathing   The
red within the black shimmers in the sun   In the cream-yellow border a shimmering
blue   From the bridge I see a huge school of small fish, farther out
perches loom, striped; when they approach, parts of the school flee toward land
Warm, moist air   A swan swims alone on the dark, still water

I see the ardor of people who now want to build the city   And who don't   .
understand the distrust, that others suspect them of wanting to build
the empire   The boat moves inside there, within a small cloud of fog suffused
with light   I have always imagined it inside a kind of Bay of Biscay
whose shores are very close in   The boat, too, is quite small
I recognize the outline of a rock in a late painting by Breugel   Or one
found in several paintings attributed to Goya, but also in a sketch for
Desastres   The architecture of the city varies   Even the Tower of
Babel grows up out of rock, in Breugel's first version   The brain's city . . .
I am in *my* European discontent   European nuclear arms are being born
The war in the Balkans continues   In the resonant fog of the European echo-chamber
genocide, its different sides, continues prismatically   The light is blinding, strikes
in all directions   I wish for an end to the killing   Only after that come the principles
of evil

CXXV

How can you,
made of shining night,
be love's jewel?

CXXVI

Enormous systems of neurons, light-connections, chemical transports
In this we are shadows of time, passing quickly   Shadows that see
Light-shadows, fire   After night comes day, then night again
We are in the process of becoming human   Nothing is instrumental

CXXVII

Destitution occurs from
the condition of God's plenum,
its equality,
to the lowliest,
their behavior
As if this were *zimzum*
in the beginning of
the Tree of the Sefiroth,
God's evacuation of himself
in order to come
to the world

and together
with humans
again
create himself

CXXVIII

Mozart's brain rests already exploded, in all its shards—

CXXIX

How can I meet you on equal terms? Only at the same eye level
But if it's impossible to calculate the position? Then we'll have to meet in the impossible
The impossible is the lowest and the highest, simultaneously, not one
                                                            after the other

CXXX

For Machiavelli, too, the greatest political crime was
the banishment, the eradication of peoples, as practiced by Philip of Macedon
The cease-fire came on the third day   Gas and electricity
have been restored in Sarajevo   The Bosnian-Serb
breakaway republic caves in, over its mass graves
What kind of peace will come? One dictated by the empire
I wish this were a defeat for the ethnic principle

and a triumph for democracy   But the contagion of darkness goes deeper
Machiavelli saw the horrors of war, his own images corresponding exactly
to television's icons, trenches full of human bodies
He pleaded for an armed peace, in readiness for a just war
to preserve the sovereign state, its empire,
because the alternative, devastation, bondage, would be worse
On what level is sovereignty defined? In what kind of violence?

Innermost in the brain death, too, exists   Its point of
crystal, dark, blinding   But death's smile
also exists   It does not yield   There are no compromises
This also pertains to music   One day music shall die—
Heart-shaped crystal, sounding, pulsating   We go off
en merveille! Or die only by slow extinction

Reduction   I am cut down from the tree, where I'm climbing, in its
finer and finer branches, sometimes near its luminous boundary   Out-
side there is darkness, the blue, darkening sphere
The tree at my side   Are we the same tree? Or a chimera?
We are not the same   Nothing has the same location, not even
in growing together   How big is your location? We move through
one another's sites   In the synaptic leap   In the ontic
For we are also hypostases, living, for one another . . .

There is the grace of shitting and the grace of pissing   We are in this
falling, toward no bottom   We fall through one another
We cannot set ourselves above anyone   Neither thieves nor murderers
Not prostitutes   Not those whose souls are evil   Not even those

who, trapped in hubris, set themselves above others   In this we are all sinners
And shall thus be stuck with our own kind   We read one another
in the single brain   Here I go again   There's no difference
The form of the brain's hubris is a kind of exclusion   Where is the formalization
that is not too rapid? Inside myself I see your love—

Do you hear the destruction of language? Yes, I hear! I hear it inside
myself, all around, everywhere   It is in its creation
In its monster form   In its highest form   I listen to this
in utmost fear   In order to find my courage   With no guarantees
Maybe it's just cowardice that hits me   But I want
to be in prayer, to what I don't know   In a song to infinity
The third trial nears its end   Then maybe
a fourth comes, and a fifth   No one knows the result
beforehand   I am in this   This is also life   This is also
confrontation   When I look death in the face, it has
no features either   But it is not the same   It is not alive

The degraded and the downtrodden   Inside me   Under the foot
of my own fear   That's where I am   Where I no longer am, even if I know
I will return, again and again   Maybe   Nothing is
the same, except for tautologies   And maybe not even there either
because according to Whitehead all functions, including logical
or mathematical, play out over time   And thus every kind of logic also
has its time, which is not eternity   Perhaps there is never any logic without
a substrate! I am the substrate   Not even Dostoevsky forgave Stavrogin
In furnaces, in hotbeds, we test the intensity of extremes   But the step
can be very small   Executioners are people   The grinding down

in the mental automata goes on without cease   Without respite
No one is immune   What is waiting for us comes regardless of our will
I will not have this! Then it's part of what is waiting for me
All the more deeply in   In what? In the invisible   What is the invisible?
There is only further penetration   Space after space   Time after time

And so peace came at last, imposed, a PAX AMERICANA
But I think: This is better than no peace at all
The alternatives are much worse   Justice will have to come later
If it comes at all   I see the stone faces of the three presidents
in front of the cameras, they don't know what to do with their hands
Light snow also fell in Dayton   From Sarajevo faces
full of joy; some people already spoke of new wars   From those
indicted for crimes against humanity no comments
I speak with A, just home from Tuzla, she has misgivings
Extensions in time   Thresholds rise clear as glass, from below
What we perceive as counterpoint, in our brains or in the real

CXXXI

Out of profound darknesses comes sleep   To be there, rocked
Watching goes on there as well   Constructs of shit   The
growing paradise   There too we wound one another—
In a painting by Georges de la Tour, Job's wife bends
over Job   Her face lit by the candle's flame   Her body
Job's face and body in darkness   She reproaches him
We're illuminated by a larger, unknown light   We are manifestations
on its surface   We look at one another   Enormities of darkness

What is it then that exists? Neither can informed un-
knowing exist   Nor can any gnostic darkness
or light   I see the angel of light   Hear the voice   Blinded
Again and again this returns   Even at the bottom of light

CXXXII

Back to the abyss   Out of which the child is born   And to which it returns
Series of song   Every single one special   Resonating out of the tradition,
which can be seen only afterward   I touch upon *themata*   Touch again
the iron vessels   Crushed, they rest   In resonating shards
I listen to the destruction of my own language   And so I'm back
in the metafunctions   What is it that I hear? That we
are being cut to bits by truth's crescent   In the deep cold
I hear a bird   The forms of pain move catatonically
The snow of comets rests on the branches of the trees   The greater tree grows
The conversation of pain   The song of pain   That which transcends affirmation
The fall is from there to the existing order   But there is no limit
The neo-liberal economies move toward full ripeness, I say
while we go for a walk   We walk through a snowy forest in severe cold
Silence, snow on the branches, small flakes are falling   My daughter brushes some
snow off her cap   We go down toward the lake, out on the ice, to
a streak of sunshine, its sparkling crystals   Walk out a bit on the ice, then
up through the oaks near Hummelmora meadow   The economies can burst
        at any time,
I say   And wonder in silence what will come flying out of the crystal-clear
                                                                    dome

We go up a hill with a view, look out over the system of suburbs, plumes of smoke
from the heating plants   Snow creaks underfoot   In the house
my mother and your mother, they both have colds   We watch the Marx Brothers
    on television,
an old black-and-white film, dated   I have seen it before   I laugh out loud
I hear Verdi's music, *Il Trovatore*, on the skidding band of sound   It is
strange, another form of sentimentality   Yet it touches me
with its enormity   The Gaussian curve of freedom, from below? Or only death
But freedom never has a probability distribution   Thus it's impossible,
does not exist; only in its overwhelming non-existence can it exist at all
Real music is much greater   We touch all the strings   Directly
Or with keys, tangents at a distance   This is how all contacts are made   Every word's

CXXXIII

The moment of brief liberation   Before one oppression
is replaced by another   In the interface between different languages
Is there a language of liberation? There is only the language of truth, its edge
Once again music from other planets is heard, in greater
expansion, in the face of a new millennium   *Jesus' blood never failed*
me yet, Bengt played for me   He should have heard this
I see his face and his head, listening-shining   Which
genocides await? He saw wickedness, evil, what
people do to one another   He tried to take his life, showed me
his bandaged wrists   For me words made their way to paper
We shall meet in a greater song   The strokes of the bow touching all the strings

CXXXIV

We listened to Mozart, an Andante grazioso, and in the new
year the Larghetto of his Piano Trio in B-flat   There I heard
modal elements I had not heard before, as in
Shostakovich, harmonic and melodic variations against a single
long, drawn-out note   I heard the astonishing boldness;
these, too, were sounds from another planet, not yet
heard by anyone   I know: Listening will go deeper and deeper
Everything's in the balance   Sometimes we can't tell night from day
You set out at dusk to buy the newspapers   I said
that you didn't have to   You fed me sections of a big orange
A black hole of monstrous dimensions has been discovered by
the Hubble Space Telescope   Its spiral-shaped dust disk has a diameter
of 300 light-years   It is 45 million light-years away from us
in the direction of the constellation Virgo, in galaxy NGC 4261   A spokesman
for the ESA talks about bizarre dynamic processes, about a titanic collision,
about a migrating black hole . . .   I read about this after my fever broke,
in a weak state   We argued later that night, sleepless
In the morning I asked you not to leave   You gave a start, your whole face changed,
and you said: Of course, I'll stay   Before falling asleep I wept   We surrender
to one another   Again I played the Mozart for you   Less
hallucinatory for me this time   No less human
Completely stiff, we touched each other   We have to break through *hubris*
The breakthrough came when I stopped waiting for you to ask
There are already cracks in the cosmology   The number of ad hoc hypotheses
grows, from the inflation model of the Big Bang to the reintroduction
of Einstein's cosmological constant, in order to prove something

entirely different   These are descriptions within existing theory
Stars considerably older than the universe are being discovered
In one star concentrations of beryllium and boron which
should not be able to exist   We are inside theory   We converse with one another
to analyze our feelings   To break through our muteness
From the high-energy research laboratory in Geneva, at CERN, comes the message
that they have produced atoms of antimatter   Thus comes

the manifestation, I

think, in real space   In the mountain's deep accelerator   In the evening
I hear on the BBC that there are nine atoms, and that now one can investigate
the characteristics of antimatter   All words are reactive, I think   There are

also

anti-words   When they encounter words annihilation occurs, to absolute energy
This feels like a historic event   That the mirror-world has
taken on real existence   That this is a new creation   Maybe this is
exaggerated   But all this is born through our inner-world . . .
Today the cold is gray, pale lavender   The trees of frost also stand waiting
I touch the girders of the destroyed language, its architecture   Its
irregular crystal forms   I move along the surfaces   Until they
come to an end   Or new asymptotes arrive   These forms are
partially fractal, partially randomized   Partially
continuous, within limits possible to integrate   From the cloud of
vectors comes a new key, C major, shining, like a new birth
The destroyed language demands unheard-of energy   Every word
is a terrifying exertion   It is I   I was there
The forms of political rhetoric move through space   They
return from the past, have altered their meaning,
in different layers of memory   Every memory is active, exists only

here, in the now   And in its projection forms   Ours is the shadow
How do we build the girders, the radial forms of shadow   In which bearing
structure, light, light, with maximum strength   Freedom
Equality   Everything else is derivative   Except love, which
is touched only by other worlds   You tell me not to cry

The logos of the degraded and downtrodden is a fiber, twined
from at least two threads   Each thread a mountain   Socrates says,
with some scorn, that he knows nothing   Then comes his demon,
the signs, the voice that speaks to him   The most de-
spised instrument is playing, in the enormous music of pain, which
I'm listening to   Hesitantly I sing along   The red banner snaps,
as when glass breaks   The taste of blood comes to my mouth   Here,
now, new degradation is born   The categories, transparent, rise out of the earth
Again anxiety about the lives of those closest to me   You reproach me
for the suffering, the pain   I answer that there is no point of comparison
Pain itself *is* this point   But I must learn better ways
to deal with the exploding anxiety, so that I do not also burn
your lives to ash   I read Socrates' parodic description of
the journey of the eleven cohorts of the gods, with all the demons in tow,
toward the highest point of heaven   How there his seriousness breaks through,
when he speaks of the super-heavenly, the *hyperuranian*   As if
for a brief moment it were accessible   To whom? To the gods? To us? What
kind of beings? Hestia alone remained below   She guarded the fire . . .
Souls remember   The journey to the super-heavenly places, or
the place, *hyperouranios topos*, also to judgment, to the correctional
facilities under the earth, the lower concentration camps . . .
Also rebirth as monsters   How the human mind

remembers this, as a remembrance of the reality of the real, which makes
the integration of the multiplicities of the senses possible . . .   The soul also
becomes a kind of Papageno, feathered all over, striving, just as laughable
as Socrates . . .   From Mexico a letter comes about the Lacandonian Rainforest,
the revolt of the Zapatistas has brought with it further felling of trees,
the army building roads everywhere, increasing narcotics traffic   As a new year's
    present
I get a figure of death, a skeleton stamped out of tin, painted white, the pelvic
arch movable with respect to the torso   Its hand wields a scythe
with a shining metallic handle, blue; the broad blade cerise   From Plato
comes the image of the body as the prison of the soul, an oyster bound in its shell
In a tunnel under the city the text: *Mozart was here! Me too*   Farther in
a middle-aged man plays a mandolin   The old woman with the clarinet is gone

Changes in justice   Above the burden, the deep droning tone   The cold
Or the warmth   Sometimes we don't know which phases we are in, con-
nected or not   Reason of state—which incessantly crushes
this justice—even though it itself ought to be grounded in justice
It very seldom is   Even in the democratic state
elitist structures are built   The intrinsic logic of state abstractions
Today in the paper I read about Ljubija, the site of mass executions, where
"the crazed greater Serbian brain buried thousands of Bosnians for
a single reason"   Every day the scientific description of the brain
                              changes
The activity of neurons can no longer be described in binary code,
rather with gradients, analogue modulations   As if there they touched
the power of the continuum   Yet every number system can be reduced
to binary opposition   As if this were the metaphysical foundation of justice   You are

either in one mode or the other   Thus the shadows grow
The demand for solidarity enters into the autistic world, into
its variation-work, and the answer comes, from inside, from the alien
world, as with an alien voice   Yes! For there are no alternatives
One cannot go against inner justice   Not without dying, inside
The fragment of the Brain draws nearer   *Cerebri substantia*
Also in its complete abstraction   Derivative   Or its
resonant information, from I-don't-know-which topologies
Hyperouranios topos   In its non-existent infinity   I hear
the music   That which cannot end   That which nonetheless has an end
That is not what's important   We are in the sound of pain   In delight; its life
With my fingers I touch your honey   I am carried by you

CXXXV

The burning thresholds come toward us hovering out of the darkness
Even in Machiavelli is the thought that killings, violent
deaths, in social conflicts distinguish themselves decisively from
their alternative, "tumults," which, as such, are fruitful for a society
In a republic   Where equality is the prerequisite for the balance of powers
And vice versa   What is growing here, now, is something else   When
society gives up its equality, from inside, there's an opening for murder
Incursions of rigidity   Fear of what is foreign   As
exists in us all, even in the innermost tenderness, Gorgonian
How do I deal with this? How to deal with reason of state in myself?
I am no better   That's why a change is possible
I see Machiavelli's song of praise to life freely lived, *il vivere libero,*

possible only in a republic, in its equality   I see its confinement
in constraint, and within universal categories   As if individuals only
existed outside the walls of the republic   Like the foreign darkness
The hierarchical states in the east were quickly transformed into
market economies   From the meltdown a new hierarchy emerges;
in part the same people at commando posts   The blood on the shadows
fades   The degraded and downtrodden rise again
in other forms   Tyranny is gone   Freedom's margins are wider
Machiavelli says that God does not want to do everything, that humans
must lend a hand   The invisible hand is almost always guided hierarchically
No value has the same name there   The struggle is identical

Allan Pettersson asked Leibowitz if he thought Bach had from the beginning
devised a structural plan, or whether he worked by instinct   The answer
was to figure that out for himself, through his own analysis . . .
There's no end to analyses   We stand at the beginning of everything
In the inner archives we are added to one another   As in bright burial chambers

CXXXVI

Recursion   In my notes I find Jewish mysticism's
concept of Language as God's Tree, ripening toward
consummation, before returning to Nothing   And we, the speakers, maybe also
singers, contributing to this process   Then I remembered my conversation with H
about Heraclitus the day before, where I disputed that for him movement
would move toward the One, asymptotically   I quoted the fragment on
there being no end to the deep logos   And saw within myself the image

of the flow, with an infinite number of fibers, voices, where each one
stood in a definite relation to, could hear the others   In growing
complexity, incessantly   A definite topological form, in the greater space
But perhaps there too is the form of ripening, the turning   The motion
of breath between everything and nothing   Then I think of the brain, the most complex
    thing
Its tree-form   The branches rise toward blue space   With a black wing
Or can this be found only in the language of the absent one   With letters of nothing
The turning of all turnings   In the form of its impossibility   It
comes nonetheless, as if from that which lies outside all reality, celestial
or terrestrial   Its mathematics is like language, with the same wounds
The same flow   The same exhalation, outside the dark mouth   That which
swallows the whole universe, all its stars   All the more narrow
We go in through the gates of the senses   To the enormous integrative flow
All discrete entities, against the contrast of the infinite background, con-
                                                    tinually
There is no image for this   It dissolves all the time   Metaphors and
metonymies form all the time   Growing clarity   Growing annihilation
Muffled drums through the walls, in what is glass-clear   Like a sub-
liminal disturbance   Or a disturbance that just manages to get through
Shrill voices   Shit music? Or the tone that alters the universe
That which exists in its increasing intensity   Until it can go no further
I have listened to human music   God's dance is in it as well
It is to people that I go   Those who exist in all their aspects
When I lie awake at night orders of forms move
inside my head, twist, turn, are permutated   I at-
tempt to remember each element, but for some there are
only gray hollows   I get up, haunt the rooms myself, take

a look   I cannot remember everything   Wonder what Bengt A would
say about what I'm at work on now   It must be fired through
The crown of darkness and of light moves, its changing form
It will feel like hunger   The brain's conflagration has no definite place
Is there no end? Of course there is   The end exists to the extent that it evades us

CXXXVII

The tree is the mountain   That which is blossoming, finely ramified
over the brow of space   The clouds are surging   The distant sound of the stars
touches us with its extinct light   It passes us,
the living   We are the thresholds   That which is form inside us
is born, like the unknown child   Then we watch over it

In the midst of this glass-clear strain I turn on the BBC
and hear that new investigations have resulted in new numbers
for the internal genocide in Cambodia   Thousands of new
mass graves have been discovered   Now they estimate
the total number of dead at about 3 million
It is late in the afternoon   This piece of news is not repeated
Later I search for it in the other media, but I don't
find it   I'm sure I was not hallucinating
Serbian exodus from Sarajevo's suburbs, in falling snow

WHO ARE THE CHILDREN OF FIRE? Those in the burning brain   Its
raging white conflagration   What rises up out of this, these whirling,
invisible flakes   We are the vessel, matrix or receptor, all children

I see floating hippocampus forms, like the horns of animals, goats or buffalo
The theory of plate tectonics is disputed, I see; fossils found in Laos
controvert notions about which parts were torn away when

from Pangaea . . .

Dicynodonts, mammal-like reptiles, the cranium's two canine teeth—
At night people light their own lights, eyes extinguished
Living they touch the dead in sleep; awake they touch the sleeping
A fractally exploding singularity   At every point living
HYPOSTASIERUNG DES VORIGEN ORBIS   No! At every point to go
against that   The connections among the living shall be almost infinite in number
UN SAISRIEN? Yes! There is no other way   The connection exists
exactly as it is established   Criticism is only possible in the next step
The infinity of potentialities incessantly explodes   There! There!
I touch your delicate brain   When I hear your voice coming   Its flowerlike

softness

I shall touch the walls of words   As if I myself were of words   And the
fine membrane, the tissue, emerged between us   On all sides
is infinity   Nor do God's variations have an ending
For Nelly Sachs each night night's wound opened with all its stars

CXXXVIII

If song is primary; who, then, is singing?

The huge image of relationships comes   All the relations of pain   All
the relations of love   How does the transformation occur? Toward what? There are
different kinds of monster attractors   The greater ocean will take back

all of its voices   Then we will see ourselves from outside   Then we will
  hear ourselves—
God's work does not wait   Nor do political forms
In the most general relationships, we are complete individuals
No language has priority   We stand amidst the boundless destruction of art
Around the throne of the invisible one stand all the names, pillars of fire
It is not I who have seen this   But it is each, each and
everyone's name, that we must not pronounce   This is the rose of fire,
even in annihilation   There are many visions   The names whirl—
If the starting point is self-delusion   The mirages,
the phantasms are what's primary   In this world contained completely
by the senses and the intellect, its delight   But even such a vision is
delusional; we don't live only in the continual expulsion
from Paradise   Boundaries are born new all the time   How to reach
vision? Machiavelli recommends the study of classical
politics combined with that of practical experience, based
on participation   Practice   Entrances   To what? He who would make
the state his Heaven makes it into Hell, says Hölderlin
Or in any case one of his fictional characters   The geometric
forms appear before our eyes   Stochastic architecture
Growing   But every small part, every increment, carries its
unique trace, in that which is subtle   As if the structure of matter were determined
by what is less than the discrete parts defined by
the physical constants, the light-thresholds in the interior . . .
Mathematical mirages   Without a doubt   Still they move ahead of us, slowly—

We went out together to look at the comet
Hyakutake, but without seeing each other we walked in different

directions; seeing you disappear toward the park on the other side of the house,
I thought I'd meet you there from the other direction   Then
you were not there, although I whistled, called out   Looked up
toward the stars, there was the crescent moon, waxing   Between
Ursa Major and the Pole Star a diffuse spot   When I raise
the binoculars I see it more clearly, a blue ball of shimmer   I can't
see the shape of the hair, it's not dark enough between the houses   When
I go in you are not there either   After a while
you come; we have sought each other out in the labyrinth of
expectations   I have read more in the book about Machiavelli   How the
multitude projects onto the prince qualities it does not possess itself
and how the prince therefore must carry off the semblance, of goodness, be-
cause with respect to evil he is no different from
other humans . . .   We carry these projections   While art
plunges deeper and deeper   In 15,000 years the comet will return, I have
read   What kinds of humans will exist then? Where will we find one another?
Mozart knew about evil   About grace   About mercy that streams
in the deep satisfaction   Enormous lightness   Enormous laughter; smiling
The second night we walked up the mountain together
to see the comet   Between the dark trees, across the snow
There! There it is   With its veil, its long hair
I had never imagined it was so long   We stand
under the constellations, our awkward projections   The moon
shines over the snow, casts moon-shadows   I see two small
shooting stars   I think of Pentti's account of a description
of Eino Leino's poetry, that it comes from infinity, reaches
a focal point of anguish, and then returns to infinity
Classical poetry has a center, family, country, the

beloved, a circle   While Leino's is a parabola   He wonders
about mine   When I first read this I felt
a knife go through me   Now I don't know   I think about the comet's orbit, its
long return   How it is up there in its silence   Its volume
bloated by the sun   I try to remember where I've read
there are comets that don't ever return   Every
moment is a focus   In superpositions of realities, real
or virtual   In overlappings of time   Maybe also
imaginary time   Then we go down the mountain   Together

But if we are the focus for love's lens   Also burning,
ravaging   You come to me with your softness, when
I least expect it   Then we are together, in passion
I was with Machiavelli in Hell   With Cesare Borgia's
butchery on the piazza at Cesena   The objects on display,
the wooden block, the bloody knife, the body cleft in two
parts, top to bottom   I think of the spilt
brain tissue, the exposed spinal cord   Political
theater, which has Machiavelli's approval   In order to main-
tain the majesty of the state   For otherwise even worse evil shall come
I have seen this before   In the world of love in all its completeness,
where Spinoza accepts with joy the sentencing of others to death
when he believes this is in consonance with God's reason . . .
The crowd's deep satisfaction in the face of the theater of cruelty
on the piazza at Cesena   As if the deep harmony were restored
Friedrich Nietzsche said he preferred the open deceit of Wagner
to guile turned inward in Brahms   But I see the man himself
in Lou Salomé's tourist snapshot, hitched like an ass to a cart

with her as the coachman, whip in hand   Did she have a whip? I hear
Don Giovanni's tense voice   I hear Sarastro   Monostatos disappearing into
the flames of night, Hell's revenge, with freedom   What is it worth?

CXXXIX

Returning   We are in the city of memory   It is creation's
first morning   A great tit is singing   I go out to
the trees, the houses, get the paper from the mailbox, lightly
rimed with frost   The sun rises behind the houses
over the snow, over human beings   That's how it always is
The brimstone butterfly and the orange underwing flew   The snow
already melting quickly, but still there in the shade   Then
I also saw a peacock butterfly, a small tortoise-shell, and a comma
Out of the abyss of politics I think   Almost nothing is
what it seems to be   The screens are called deception, self-
deception, individual or collective   Hell's
forms move   Verily we shall be with one another
in Paradise   I finish reading the book on Shostakovich; it
presents a crushed man; except when in deep concentration,
where he is in music, in his ultimate seriousness, despair
I think about the forms of the hippocampus, the art of fixing memories   That
new thoughts are as dreams; if they are not quickly ob-
jectified, they disappear   I touch the blinding sound
I try to phone my mother, who has pneumonia
but there's a busy signal   I understand, that in the great listening
I shall hear voices, the voice ahead of me   Even if listening

is simultaneous through all time   About music and violence; in this
impossibility   Everything simultaneous; in this love   Now
the voices are summed   Even the voices of the dead come from in front, as from
an infinite absence   But all music comes out of this infinity
Listening-receiving   Total reality such as it comes to me
The unheard-of, potential, imaginary world of sound   Of which
mathematics is only a small part   Or vice versa   There is no
difference   We are listening-inward   That which comes into actuality
comes with its blinding   Or with its satisfaction, its delight

CXL

The inner shadow forms superimposed   Virtual or imaginary
As in the interior of matter   What is matter? No one knows   But ignorance
is never knowledge; in contrast to the cognizance of it . . .
What kind of delicate walls does Mozart's third brain have? What
kind of transparency   What kind of permeability,
as if it were the membrane to infinity . . .
Just so time sieves through us, as if it were
an independent substance, but it is not
Time is born out of us, as our child, by infinity
The *apokatastasis* of all brains, simultaneously   As in an
                                        unheard-of
cosmic blossoming—   In its complete simultaneity; immobile
Now   Now the monster is coming   What is beheld; by all the senses
Each one alone steers   By his own alien stars

Battles in Lebanon   Air attacks, hundreds of thousands of people in
flight   Katyusha rockets against Israel   *This has no end*
I read in Ibn Arabi about the concept of *ittihad*, the union
of incompatible essences in the one, a false doctrine, and about
the abyss that separates this from love's being . . .
I am He whom I love, He whom I love is I, says
al-Hallaj   As if this had reality only in God
About this one can read in *The Book of Annihilation*
Nada   Nada   That which is in the cloud of the annihilation of knowledge

Last night in a dream I touched an infinity-computer   I
used it; was also used by it   Simultaneously I was outside
it; it was smaller than I   It hovered in my inner space
What did it compute? It was the whole universe   I remembered this
It computed the infinities   It used them as numbers
The instantaneous moves   There is no difference   Touch
me! Every word's touch is lightning-quick   Afterward everything's changed
I shall be in stringency   Even where everything goes wrong, is compromised
How will I break through? Maybe it won't be noticed either, not at all

CXLI

Mozart's third brain is unfinished, I grasp this over and over
                                                again
I cannot learn   The need for completion is
enormous, leads to blinding after blinding, even

when one believes oneself amidst revelation　But you
touch me　I touch you　Our bodies are mortal
Gödel's ladder has no summit　It bears the crown of nothing
Don Giovanni, as he moves in his inner constraint, into death
The demonic music plays　What was a butterfly form
touches the great darkness　What occurred was murder　There was no
barrier　The great movements stirring within the peoples　*Viva
la libertà!* Also resonant of genocide　Women's
faces　Their pudenda　Narrowness　Widening　Light-
forms; blinding; or mild, not-blinding　You
bear the acqueous form of your voice, its flowerlike clarity, soft
Its inner edge, far beyond pain　Alive there

CXLII

I played the flute　The underworld of the fugue stood open
　　　　　　　　Out there the armies are waiting,
the creatures of blinding night　What are we waiting for?
I was very happy　Lightness is touching me . . .

But movement simultaneously comes from a hidden
third world　It has no name　It
doesn't let itself be named　Then it vanishes
Around every structure is the invisible cloud of
other structures　Where is the selection made? By whom?
By no one? That's highly probable　We are
stochastic entities　We bear our own darkness

Superposition   In the black notebook I
left on a subway car at Times Square on its way
to Queens, there is something about the connection
between Leibniz's monads and virtual states at
the quantum level   Communication? Aspect's action-at-a-distance, extended
across the whole universe . . .   The notebook has existed for a long
time in pure virtuality   Can it be called back? No! Not even
if we all try at once   The light cone for each event in the universe
is bent by gravitation, I read   Thus all geometry is non-Euclidean,
I think   According to Penrose, speculatively, this might also
apply to virtual events, and there, only there, would the cones'
tilt be able to grow so large that some timelines would close, Gödel-
                                        Cosmologically . . .

With the flute shrilling I leap
between the mountains   Out toward the cry of the sun—

CXLIII

GRAN DISPARATE   Someone holds his own decapitated head,
his other hand feeds it with a spoon   Someone else pours
liquid down a funnel into the throat hole in the trunk; blood
or wine; from a jug with a handle   For the heart?
The gray shadow of a female figure watches this from behind—

In the Kyrie of the great, unfinished Mass in C minor
the voices come in from enormity with their full humanity

as if by doing so they constituted enormity   As
toward the end of *Don Giovanni*, I say   Yes, you
answer   We move in silence   Out there is the white light of June

The tulips stand in their beauty   Lift their chalices
up toward the white light   Pink-orange-red ones, doubled
Small ones, red, the inner edges of their petals fringed, turned
inward   The big yellow ones, radiant   I look into their bottoms,
their different fields, yellow-green, blue, black, powdered over
                                                with pollen—

CXLIV

The shadows of the third brain   Light from all directions
Light   Backlight   Time   Countertime   The sounds go against
one another   Interference   Annihilation   Amplification   We are
this light   Also in its form of darkness   There is no end

The white light blows through the trees   Infin-
ity sings   We don't hear it   It does not exist
It sings its lullaby   For us   For us
We sing for infinity   For one another—

On the path in the woods lies a small blue egg, speckled brown,
broken   On one part of the inside, where the white membrane no longer is,
it shines clear blue, in its inner vault   Here the song ends—

NOTES

Göran Sonnevi wrote *Mozart's Third Brain* between 3 July 1992 and 12 June 1996. The notes that follow, many more than in the Swedish edition, have been appended over a longer period of time.

I

Valfjället: a rocky eminence on the island of Koster (off Sweden's west coast, in the Skagerrak) on which signal fires were probably lit.

IV

hapseis: plural of *hapsis*, Greek for touch, connection, contact. The word is used in Plato's dialogue *Parmenides* to represent hypothetical connections between distinct entities in the one. The same root can be found in "synapse," from New Latin *synapsis* (from Greek), a junction, connection; *syn-*, together + *hapsis*, a joining < *haptein*, to join.

Torsten Renqvist (1924–2007): Swedish artist, known chiefly for his sculpture.

to exaiphnes: Greek, the instantaneous; used in Plato's *Parmenides*. (Also in XXIII.)

VI

Die Vernichtung der Juden Lettlands. Churbn Lettland: The Destruction of the Jews of Latvia by Max Kaufmann (Munich, 1947) was self-published under the auspices of the American military government GEC-AGO, EUCOM (European Command) in July 1947. It is an eye-witness account of the annihilation of Latvian Jewry. The original edition is 542 pages long, in German with a few portions in English and in Yiddish, and contains a few photographs. An English translation of the book, by Laimdota Mazzarins, is posted at http://jewsoflatvia.com/.

XIV

dulce et decorum est pro patria mori: Horace *Odes* 3.2.13. Sweet and proper it is to die for one's country.

XXV

Bengt Anderson: 17 July 1935–4 October 1993.
    polytropoi anthropoi: Greek, people of many turnings. Compare the epithet for Odysseus, *polytropos andros*, "the man of twists and turns" (Fagles, trans.).

XXVI

amechanos: Greek, awkward.
    Kullaberg: See note to CIV.

XXVIII

Pallas Athana: Pallas Athena, Doric spelling in Pindar.

XXIX

"torches of the dark mullein" or "the mullein's dark torches" refer to *Verbascum nigrum*, dark mullein—in Swedish, *mörkt kungsljus*.

XXX

"velvet boletes": Swedish *sammetssopp*, *Xerocomus subtomentosus*; their caps are velvety and can vary from gray-green to brownish yellow to a warm chocolate brown.

XXXV

Sir Andrzej Panufnik's *Arbor Cosmica* consists of twelve Evocations for twelve strings, all generated from a single three-note chord mapped like a tree.
    Giacinto Scelsi's String Quartet no. 5 dates from 1985; its composition was precipitated by the death of the composer's close friend the poet Henri Michaux (1899–1984).
    "reduced to humility by disaster": The phrase is from Michaux's poem "Clown," which Anderson and Sonnevi knew in a translation by Erik Lindegren and Ilmar Laaban.

XLIII

Anna R: The Swedish poet Anna Rydstedt (22 April 1928–4 July 1994), whose poems, collected in *Anna Rydstedt: Dikter,* edited by Göran Sonnevi and Jan Olov Ullén, appeared from Bonniers in the fall of 2000. (Also in XLVII and other parts of the poem.)

XLVII

Ventlinge: village on the southwest coast of Öland, a Baltic island off the southeast coast of Sweden.

Gustaf Dannstedt: Anna Rydstedt's husband.

LVI

Nelson Mandela: The indirect quotation given in the Swedish text has been rendered here. Mandela's exact words were: "Never, never and never again shall it be that this beautiful land will again experience the oppression of one by another and suffer the indignity of being the skunk of the world."

LX

Virgin Mary's keys: (Swedish *Jungfru Marie nycklar*) *Dactylorhiza*—formerly *Orchis—maculata,* whose common English name is heath spotted orchid.

St. Peter's keys: (Swedish *Sankte Pers nycklar*) *Orchis mascula,* in English commonly called male orchis or early purple orchid.

LXIII

Alvar: Tracts of limestone steppe, known as the Alvar, cover large areas of Öland. Here thin layers of alkaline soil, in which calcicolous plants grow, are interspersed with limestone outcroppings. Sonnevi's "Alvar" is the so-called Big Alvar, which covers about one quarter of Öland.

LXV

flower fly: See note to LXXI.

LXVI

hoi polloi kakoi: Greek, the bad many/multitude/masses. Citation from Plato's *Republic* (490d). Also in a fragment of Heraclitus (104, Diels).

LXXI

flower fly: Here, as in LXV, the poet uses *blomsterflugor* interchangeably with *blomflugor*, flies of the family Syrphidae, with about 5,500 species, more than three hundred of which are found in Sweden. They are generally called hover flies in English. Most feed on nectar, and they are often seen on flowers. Their big eyes seem to cover their entire heads. Many mimic the appearance of bees or wasps.

Family Aeschnidae (or Aeshnidae): A family of relatively large hawker dragonflies. Most of the European species belong to the genus *Aeshna*. In North America members of this family are called darners; they are brilliant blue, green, or brown insects with large clear wings and are among the largest and fastest flying dragonflies.

- *Aeschna grandis* is easily distinguished by its amber wing membrane; the female lacks blue spots at front of abdomen. Its English common name is brown hawker.
- emperor dragonfly: *Anax imperator*, Swedish *kejsar(troll)slända*.

Family Corduliidae: A family of medium-sized hawkers or skimmers with metallic bodies, usually bronze or green.

- regal gold-ringed dragonfly: my translation for Sonnevi's *kungsslända*, an alternate for *kungstrollslända: Cordulegaster boltonii*, whose common English name is common goldenring.
- gold skimmer (common English name downy emerald): *Cordulia aenea*, Swedish *guld(troll)slända*.

Family Libellulidae: A large family of darters or skimmers.

Family Agriidae: A family, mainly tropical, with three European species, consisting of the largest damselflies, broad-winged damselflies.

- blue broad-winged damselflies (common English name beautiful demoiselle): *Agrion (Calopteryx) virgo*, Swedish *blå jungfruslända*.

Family Coenagriidae: A large family of damselflies.

- a red damselfly: Swedish *röd flickslända*, most likely the large red damselfly, *Pyrrhosoma nymphula*.

gray hawkweeds: *Hieracium pilosella*, Swedish *gråfibblor*, in English called mouse-ear hawkweed.

LXXIV

horva: In *Anna Rydstedt: Dikter* (see note to XLIII) Rydstedt's gloss on *horva* reads: "small enclosed field or meadow; small pasture land; partitioning of a village's common land outside the village or behind a [farmer's] garden.—More and more *horva* has come to mean a small piece of land. Its most widespread use is on Öland and in Småland."

LXXVIII

Kerylos: The male of the halcyon species. In fragment 26 Alkman also writes of the female, the *Alkyon.* (Also see XCIII.)

LXXXIX

haptic: See note to IV.

XC

social group: a group of persons who form a relatively homogeneous unit in social status. The term *socialgrupp* more or less replaced *socialklass* as a concept during the heyday of the welfare state. There were three numbered social groups, roughly corresponding to the upper, middle, and lower classes.

XCII

ANAX, ANASSA: Greek, ruler or sovereign; master, mistress, respectively.

kitharodoi: plural of Greek *kitharodos,* one who sings to the kithara (Latin/English: cithara), an ancient Greek stringed instrument of the lyre class whose soundbox was made of wood.

XCV

Fredman, brothers, sisters: In *Fredman's Epistles* (1790) and *Fredman's Songs* (1791), the Swedish poet and musician Carl Michael Bellman (1740–1795) celebrated the lives and exploits of the imaginary Fredman (a renowned Stockholm watchmaker fallen on hard times) and his companions in the vine, the "brothers" and "sisters" of the Order of Bacchus.

XCVI

This section opens with a reference to Sophocles' *polla ta deina kouden anthropou deinoteron pelei*, the start of the second choral entrance in *Antigone*. English renditions of the Sophocles tend to present variations on Sir Richard Jebb's sense of this line as "Wonders are many   And none is more wonderful than man." Sonnevi, like Hölderlin (who translated this as: *Ungeheuer ist viel. Doch nichts / Ungeheuerer, als der Mensch*), touches down on the more monstrous side of the duality of *deinos*, which means not only fearful/dreadful/terrible/awesome but also fantastic/wondrous/marvelous/ strange, giving us *vidunderlig* for the Greek *deinos*, German *ungeheuer*. My rendition was monstrously tipped toward the end of this section, where Sonnevi writes of the movement of the monsters (*vidundren*), of their dance, which calls to mind Paul Klee's *Tanze Du Ungeheuer zu meinem sanften Lied*.

C

Gallows Hill: See note to CIV.

CI

The birth comes monstrously: Concerning "monstrous," see note to XCVI.

The Book of the Thorn Rose (or The Book of the Wild Rose, *Törnrosens bok*)— something of a *Gesamtkunstwerk* consisting of fourteen volumes published in two different editions between 1832 and 1851—encompassed a great many novels, stories, plays, poems, essays, and works in mixed genres by the Swedish author Carl Jonas Love Almqvist (1793–1866). Also see note to CXXIV.

CIII

Nissan: The river that flows through Halmstad, also referred to (though not by name) in CV.

CIV

The land- and seascapes in this section are around Halmstad, a city on the west coast of Sweden, in the province of Halland, where Sonnevi grew up. Gallows Hill (Swedish Galgberget) is north of downtown Halmstad; about 150 years ago gallows surmounted its crest. The hospital where the poet's mother (and father) died is just below its crest, with a view toward the sea.

Hallands Väderö, which Sonnevi refers to as Väderön, is an island nature reserve in the Kattegat, an arm of the North Sea between Sweden and Denmark. Torekov is a town on the mainland's Bjäre peninsula, somewhat south of Hallands Väderö. Kullaberg (also called Kullen) is a rocky hill on a point of land that juts out into the Kattegat even farther south along the coast. Laxvik is on the coast just south of Halmstad. Lagan, a river, empties into the bay of Laholm, south of Laxvik, but northeast of the places mentioned above.

CV

libero arbitrio: free will.

CVI

Ljusnan: One of the large rivers of Norrland that runs from Härjedalen, near the Norwegian border, continuing through Hälsingland, and emptying out into the Baltic Sea.

Karl, *Aftonbladet*: See note to CVII.

CVII

Karl Vennberg (11 April 1910–12 May 1995): Swedish author known chiefly for his fifteen books of poetry and for his criticism. In the 1960s he served as cultural editor for *Aftonbladet*, one of Sweden's afternoon newspapers. He is also referred to, though not by name, in LVIII and LXXIV.

CVIII

Hölderlin's thought: In current Swedish editions the phrase is "Hölderlin's dictum." The formulation *Das Werden im Vergehen*—rendered as "Becoming in Dissolution" by Thomas Pfau, translator and editor of *Friedrich Hölderlin: Essays and Letters on Theory*—is a title given by *editors* to a prose fragment in various editions of Hölderlin's works. The title encapsulates these basic concepts and their interrelatedness within the fragment.

fritillarias: *Fritillaria meleagris* (English guinea-hen flower or simply fritillary),

Swedish *kungsängslilja*, so called because of their rich occurrence in Kungsängen, near Uppsala.

cowslips: *Primula veris*, Swedish *gullviva*; the flowers are usually yellow, but in older gardens, over time, some will have red flowers.

CIX

conifer false morel: *Gyromitra esculenta*, Swedish *stenmurkla*, has brainlike convolutions.

black morels: *Morchella elata*, Swedish *toppmurkla*, has a dark-ribbed honeycombed cap that is elongate and narrowly conical. It may be a complex of practically indistinguishable varieties. Although *Morchella elata* are called black morel in English, the colors of their caps and ribs vary greatly.

CXI

Ormöga is a village on Öland, a Baltic island off the southeast coast of Sweden. The name translates literally as Snake Eye.

CXII

night-scented orchids (or night orchid): (Swedish *nattviol*) *Platanthera bifolia*, lesser butterfly orchid. Here Sonnevi describes both the lesser butterfly orchid (*P. bifolia*) and the greater butterfly orchid (*P. chlorantha*): the Swedish plural, *nattvioler*, takes both under its wing.

fragrant orchids: *Gymnadenia conopsea*, Swedish *brudsporre*.

fly orchids: *Ophrys insectifera*, Swedish *flugblomster*.

early marsh orchids: *Dactylorhiza incarnata*, Swedish *ängsnycklar*.

burnt orchids: *Orchis ustulata*, Swedish *krutbrännare*.

CXIII

musk orchid: *Herminium monorchis*, Swedish *honungsblomster* (literally "honey blossom").

dwarf thistle: *Cirsium acaule*, Swedish *jordtistel* (literally "earth thistle").

wild roses: *Rosa canina*, Swedish *vildrosor*.

CXIV

already dead: In the poem "Fagerfjäll, Tjörn, 1986; For Pentti" (see *A Child Is Not a Knife*, 62–63), Sonnevi addresses the great twentieth-century Finnish poet Pentti Saarikoski in similar words when Saarikoski is asked by a Finnish political party to be its candidate for minister of culture. Also see note to CXXXVIII.

CXV

Alvar: See note to LXIII.
   butterworts: *Pinguicula vulgaris*, Swedish *tätört*.
   marsh helleborine: an orchid, *Epipactis palustris*, Swedish *kärrknipprot*.
   Blue libellulas: see note to LXXI. Here Sonnevi refers to *Orthetrum cancellatum*; only the mature male is blue; the young male resembles the female.
   lacertines: (Swedish *drakslingor*) A term used to describe a lizardlike, serpentine, or dragonlike depiction or ornament, occurring individually or as an element in an animal interlace. These lacertines are on the runestones.
   rock-roses: *Helianthemum nummularium*, Swedish *solvända*.

CXVII

Vänneböke: A village in western Småland, close to the border of Halland.
   Torekov: The poet is back on the west coast of Sweden; see note to CIV.
   Ormöga: See CXI (and note) and CXIV.

CXIX

cloudberries: *Rubus chamaemorous*, Swedish *hjortron*.
   bog asphodel: *Narthecium ossifragum*, Swedish *myrlilja*.
   cross-leaved heath: *Erica tetralix*, Swedish *klockljung*.
   bog myrtle (or sweet gale): *Myrica gale*, Swedish *pors*.

CXXII

Dsha tele: The early-twentieth-century Danish cultural historian Frederik Troels-Lund writes in *Dagligt Liv in Norden i det 16:e Aarhundrede* (Daily life in the Nordic countries in the sixteenth century) of the Romany phrase *dsha tele*. It comes from a Gypsy song about preparing for death and in context means "Go down [to the underworld]."

CXXIV

Lövholmen, Kofsan: Small islands in Mälaren, one of Sweden's large lakes, near the poet's home.

henbane: *Hyoscyamus niger*, Swedish *bolmört*.

my European discontent: A reference to Almqvist's *Europeiska missnöjets grunder* (The bases for European discontent), a radical political essay on social change including women's emancipation, included in *Törnrosens bok*. See note to CI.

CXXX

We go off / *en merveille!*: A reference to a mystical erotic dream (23–24 April 1744) in Swedenborg's *Dream Diary*.

CXXXIII

Jesus' blood never failed / me yet: A composition by the English composer Gavin Bryars (b. 1943) that loops, plays, and replays this simple refrain.

CXXXVII

HYPOSTASIERUNG DES VORIGEN ORBIS: Hypostasization of the previous orbit.
UN SAISRIEN: A know-nothing.
Both are quotations from Hölderlin's fragmentary hymn "Columbus."

CXXXVIII

Pentti Saarikoski (1937–1983): Finnish poet, classical scholar, and translator of Homer's *Odyssey*, James Joyce's *Ulysses*, and many other works. In the language of his own poetry and the various idioms he devised for his translations, Saarikoski made Finnish literary language responsive to the cadences and syntax of the vernacular. See also note to CXIV.

Eino Leino (1878–1926): Finnish poet, critic, novelist, journalist, translator of Dante's *Divine Comedy* and much else. Bringing to it elements from the *Kalevala* along with its own body of folk songs as well as attributes from the poetry of the Nordic countries and the continent, Leino transformed Finnish poetic language.

CXXXIX

brimstone butterfly: *Gonepteryx rhamni*, Swedish *citronfjäril*.
    orange underwing: *Archiearis parthenias*, Swedish *brun flickfjäril*.
    peacock butterfly: *Inachis io*, Swedish *påfågelsöga*.
    small tortoise-shell: *Aglais urticae*, Swedish *nässelfjäril*.
    comma: *Polygonia c-album*, Swedish *vinbärsfuks*.

CXL

apokatastasis: restitution, restoration; from Greek *apokathistemi*, to restore, to reestablish. The word is used in Acts 3:21.
    Ibn Arabi (1165–1240): Sufi mystic-philosopher who was born in Valencia and died in Damascus. He was the author of over four hundred books, among them *The Book of Annihilation*.
    al-Hallaj (858–922): Regarded as the greatest of the early Sufi mystics, he was gruesomely martyred in Baghdad. In current Swedish editions of *Mozart's Third Brain*, the citation from al-Hallaj translates literally as "I am He who loves, He who loves am I." The English rendition is the accurate one.

BIBLIOGRAPHY

Göran Sonnevi is the author of fifteen books of poems and a volume of poetry in translation; he has supervised three collections of earlier volumes. A selection of his work by Marie Silkeberg (*Dikter i urval av Marie Silkeberg*) came out from Bonniers in March 2008. These fifteen books, some in combination with others, since 1982 have also been issued as mass-market paperbacks.

Sonnevi's Books in Swedish (Published by Bonniers)

Outfört (Unrealized), 1961.
Abstrakta dikter (Abstract poems), 1963.
ingrepp—modeller (intervention—models), 1965.
och nu! (and now!), 1967.
Det gäller oss. Dikter 1959–1968 (This concerns us: Poems, 1959–1968), 1969.
Det måste gå (It has to work), 1970.
Det oavslutade språket (The unfinished language), 1972.
Dikter 1959–1973 (Poems, 1959–1973), 1974.
Det omöjliga (The impossible), 1975.
Språk; Verktyg; Eld (Language; Tools; Fire), 1979.
Dikter 1959–1972, rev. utg. (Revised edition of Poems, 1959–1973), 1981.
Små klanger; en röst (Small chimes; one voice), 1981.
Dikter utan ordning (Poems with no order), 1983.
Oavslutade dikter (Unfinished poems), 1987.
Trädet (The tree), 1991.
Framför ordens väggar. Dikter i översättning 1959–1992 (Poems in translation, 1959–1992), 1992.

Mozarts Tredje Hjärna (Mozart's third brain), 1996.
Klangernas bok (The book of sounds), 1998.
Oceanen (The ocean), 2005.
Dikter i urval av Marie Silkeberg, 2008.

Translations

In addition to the book-length collections listed chronologically (also under each language) below, translations of Sonnevi's poetry have appeared in Arabic, Bulgarian, Catalan, Chinese, English, Greek, Hungarian, Kurdish, Malayalam, Polish, Portuguese, Russian, Serbo-Croat, Slovak, and an Indian language the author cannot identify. For details concerning slimmer English selections, please consult the bibliography in *A Child Is Not a Knife*.

Translations of Sonnevi's Poetry into Various Languages (Volumes)

In French

Et maintenant! Trans. François-Noël Simoneau. Honfleur: Oswald, 1970.

In Finnish

Keskeneräinen kieli. Trans. Pentti Saarikoski. Helsinki, Otava, 1977, 2nd ed. 2006.
Valtameri. Trans. Jyrki Kiiskinen. Helsinki: Tammi, 2007.

In Turkish

Şiirler. Trans. Lütfi Özkök and Yavuz Çekirge. Istanbul: Yeditepe, 1978.

In Dutch

Het Onmogelijke en andere gedichten. Trans. Lisette Keustermans and Leo Wilders. Afterword Lisette Keustermans. Ghent: Masereelfonds, 1983.
Het geluidenboek. Trans. Lisette Keustermans. Leuven: Uitgeverij P, 2009.

In Icelandic

Mál; Verkfæri; Eldur. Trans. Sigurður A. FriðÞjófsson. Iceland: Svart á hvítu, 1986.

In German

Das Unmögliche: Gedichte 1958–75. Trans. Klaus-Jürgen Liedtke. Münster: Kleinheinrich, 1988.
Sprache; Werkzeug; Feuer: Gedichte 1975–87. Trans. Klaus-Jürgen Liedtke. Münster: Kleinheinrich, 1989.
Das brennende Haus. Trans. Klaus-Jürgen Liedtke. Munich: Hanser Verlag, 2009.

In Spanish

Poemas sin terminar. Trans. Roberto Mascaró. Montevideo: Coedition Vinten Editor Siesta, 1991.
Que trata de nosotros. Trans. Francisco J. Uriz. Vitoria-Gasteiz: Ediciones Bassarai, 2000.

In English

A Child Is Not a Knife: Selected Poems of Göran Sonnevi. Trans. Rika Lesser. Princeton, NJ: Princeton University Press, 1993.

In Norwegian

Et ansikt. Dikt i utvalg. Trans. Geir Gulliksen. Oslo: Forlaget Oktober, 1995.

In Danish

Et usynligt træ. Digte 1981–1996. Trans. Karsten Sand Iversen. Århus: Husets Forlag, 1999.

In Romanian

Cartea sunetelor. Trans. Gabriela Melinescu. Bucharest: Editura Univers, 2000.

In Italian

Variazioni mozartiane ed altre poesie. Trans. Bruno Argenziano. Florence: Pagliai Polistampa, 2006.

ACKNOWLEDGMENTS

Thanks to the editors of the following publications, in which numbered sections of *Mozart's Third Brain* or a few of its *Disparates* first appeared, as follows:

Barrow Street: XXXVII–XLI and LXXI
Cipher Journal (Internet magazine): LVI, LXV, LXVI, LXIX
Circumference: LIII
The Dirty Goat: CIX–CX, CXVII–CXXVII
Electronic Poetry Review (Internet magazine): CVI, CVII, CXI, CXII, CXIV, CXV, CXVI, CXXVIII, CXXIX, CXXX
Fourteen Hills: XXXII, XXXIII, XXXV, XXXVI
Guernica: A Magazine of Art and Politics (Internet magazine): XVI–XVIII, XLIX, LIX, LXXXV, LXXXVIII
Göran Sonnevi. Poesifestival i Nässjö (publication following the 2000 Poetry Festival in Sweden): VII
Literary Imagination: I, II, III, IV
Manhattan Review: XLII, L, LI
Metamorphoses: V, XIII, XV
Natural Bridge: VII, VIII, IX
The Paris Review: XXXIV
Partisan Review: "There shall be life . . ." and LIV
Pequod: CXXXIV–CXLIV
Pleiades: LXXXI
Poetry: CV
Scandinavian Review: LXXIX, LXXXIII, LXXXIV, LXXXVI, LXXXIX, XCVI
Seneca Review: X, XI, XII

Swedish Book Review: XIV, XIX–XXI, and XLIII–XLVII
Taiga: LXXV, LXXVI, LXXVII
Threepenny Review: LXVIII
TriQuarterly: XLVIII
TWO LINES: Crossings: XXII, XXIII, XXIV; *TWO LINES: Bodies:* XCV; *TWO LINES: Wherever I Lie Is Your Bed:* XCVIII
Typo (Internet magazine): LXIV, LXXX, LXXXII, LXXXVII, CVIII, CXIII; XC–XCIV
Western Humanities Review: VI, XXV–XXVIII
Words Without Borders—The Online Magazine for International Literature: LV, LVII, LVIII, LX, LXI, LXVII, LXX, and CIV

Without assistance in the form of fellowships, grants or awards from the Fulbright Commission, the National Endowment for the Arts, *Sveriges författarfond*, and the Swedish Institute, I could not have embarked on or completed the translation of this poem; I am deeply grateful for each of them. Thanks, also, to the American-Scandinavian Foundation for recognizing my work on Sonnevi again with the 2002 Translation Prize for a selection of poems from this manuscript.

Over the course not only of the last decade of work on this book but the quarter century of work on Sonnevi, Swedish friends or friends made in Sweden inspired, cajoled, or distracted me, as necessary. Some are no longer living—Bengt Andersson, Ingrid Ekelöf, Berndt Petterson, Leif Sjöberg, Joan Tate, Göran Tunström; many still are—Maj Andersson, Anna Birbrajer, Aldo Bolle, Lena Cronqvist, Catherine Sandbach Dahlström, Suzanne Kolare, Nancy Miller, Gina Riddle, Kaj Schueler, Tomas and Monica Tranströmer, Birgitta Trotzig. Every one was immensely helpful, and I offer heartfelt thanks.

On this side of the Atlantic I want to acknowledge gratitude for my two closest readers, who believe everything I say about Swedish, Richard Howard and Rosanna Warren, and for George C. Schoolfield, Professor Emeritus at Yale, and his long fellowship in the language and literature. Many friends were subjected to repeated drafts or technical queries, to name the handful my brain remembers best—my sister Joan Japha, Dominic Kinsley, Kathrin Perutz, Ed Rothstein, and Paul O. Zelinsky; there are not enough words for thanks. Lawrence Joseph, Mark Rudman, C. K. Williams, and Adam Zagajewski have been particular champions of *Mozart's Third Brain*; much obliged for spreading the word in more ways than one.

As ever, to the Sonnevis, for the coffee, the mushrooms, the work, the walks, the friendship that endures every weather, and the smiles: *Tack. Tack så väldigt mycket!*

AUTHOR INFORMATION

Biography: Göran Sonnevi

Born in Lund, Sweden, on 3 October 1939, Göran Sonnevi spent his childhood and youth in Halmstad, where he studied the natural sciences, concentrating in mathematics. From 1958 to 1966 he attended the University of Lund, where he studied the humanities. In 1966 he moved to Järfälla, now a part of the greater Stockholm metropolitan area, where he continues to live and write.

Among his many awards are the Bonniers Literary Magazine Prize, 1967; Swedish Radio's Poetry Prize, 1968; *Aftonbladets* Literature Prize, 1972; the Aniara Prize, 1975; and both the Swedish Academy's Bellman Prize and *Svenska Dagbladet*'s Literary Prize in 1979. In 1983 Sonnevi became a recipient of a lifetime grant from the Swedish government, bestowed on 125 artists in honor of their contributions to the nation's culture. His more recent honors include: in 1997 the Östrabo Prize of Småland's Academy (in memory of the poet Esaias Tegnér) and the Gerard Bonniers Prize of the Swedish Academy; in 1998 the Erik Lindegren Prize and the Ferlin Prize (the first from Luleå commune, the second from the Nils Ferlin Society); in 2005 the Nordic Prize from the Swedish Academy, known as "the little Nobel"; and the 2006 Literature Prize of the Nordic Council.

On 4 October 2007 Göran Sonnevi became the proud grandfather of Vilgot, son of Anna. Kerstin Sonnevi (née Kronkvist), whom he married in 1961, now retired from teaching elementary schoolchildren, is the delighted and doting grandmother.

Biography: Rika Lesser

Born in Brooklyn, New York, on 21 July 1953, Rika Lesser took an early interest in the sciences but graduated from Yale University with a BA summa cum laude in 1974. She holds an MFA from Columbia University School of the Arts (Writing, 1977). She is the author of four collections of poetry, *Etruscan Things* (Braziller, 1983), *All We Need of Hell* (North Texas, 1995), *Growing Back* (South Carolina, 1997), and *Questions of Love: New and Selected Poems* (Sheep Meadow, 2008). She has translated and published collections of poetry by Göran Sonnevi, Gunnar Ekelöf, and Claes Andersson, as well as Rainer Maria Rilke and Hermann Hesse (including *Siddhartha: An Indic Poem*, Barnes and Noble Classics, 2007). She also translates books for children and readers of all ages from Swedish and German.

Rika Lesser has been the recipient of the Amy Lowell Travelling Poetry Scholarship (1974–1975), an Ingram-Merrill Foundation Award for Poetry Writing (1978–1979), fellowships from the Fulbright Foundation (1999) and the National Endowment for the Arts (2001), the Harold Morton Landon Translation Prize from the Academy of American Poets (1982), the Poetry Translation Prize of the Swedish Academy (1996), and other awards. The American-Scandinavian Foundation gave her its Translation Prize twice— in 1992 for selections from Sonnevi's *A Child Is Not a Knife*, and in 2002 for selections from *Mozart's Third Brain*. Lesser teaches poetry and literary translation and has long made Brooklyn Heights her home.